THE REFORM OF RENEWAL

FR. BENEDICT J. GROESCHEL, C.F.R.

THE REFORM OF RENEWAL

IGNATIUS PRESS   SAN FRANCISCO

The photograph on the back cover
shows the Franciscan Sisters and
Franciscan Friars of the Renewal
gathered on the steps of St. Crispin's friary
in the South Bronx on April 2, 1990,
the day of their canonical establishment
by John Cardinal O'Connor, Archbishop of New York.
Father Groeschel is the first friar on the left.

Cover art: St. Clare of Assisi by John Lynch
Cover design by Riz Boncan Marsella

With ecclesiastical approval
© 1990 Ignatius Press, San Francisco
ISBN 0-89870-286-0
Library of Congress catalogue number 90-81769
Printed in the United States of America

To Some Great Women of Reform from the Past:

CLARE OF ASSISI
CATHERINE OF SIENA
CATHERINE OF GENOA
TERESA OF AVILA

and of the present:

MOTHER TERESA
MOTHER PAULA
MOTHER ANGELICA
CATHERINE DOHERTY
DOROTHY DAY

CONTENTS

FOREWORD

Religious sociologists today speak of the new voluntarism as one of the most significant religious changes in American churches. Today we are confronted with a radically individualistic religiosity. Choice means more than simply selecting which church one will belong to; choice involves religion itself as an option as well as the opportunity to draw selectively from a variety of traditions in pursuit of the self. Questions of authority, discipline, religious practice and common life often seem foreign, or at least unimportant.

Robert Bellow, in one of his books, characterizes the modern American religious experience in the person of Sheila Larson who says: "I believe in God. I'm not a religious fanatic. I can't remember the last time I went to church. My faith has carried me a long way. It's Sheilaism. Just my own little voice."

Father Benedict's sound Catholic ecclesiology offers an antidote to the rampant individualism that has invaded American religiosity and that is so foreign to the communal aspect of Catholicism which includes our communion with our ancestors in the faith, "the host of witnesses" stretching back to the apostles and martyrs. The mystery of the Church, the guiding presence of the Spirit in the Magisterium, the legacy of holiness in our saints and heroes are all part of the backdrop for personal conversion and community change that mean reform.

As Pope John Paul II points out in *Christifideles Laici,* our

Catholic people are commissioned by their baptism and
confirmation to transform society. Father Benedict echoes
this challenge in the opening chapters. The relative prosperity of the last twenty-five years has induced a flabby, comfortable religion that fails to face the conflict between time
and eternity. The mediocrity of these times cries out for
reform. Our author explores various areas of Christian
living which apply to all believers, lay and religious, and
which are key aspects of an authentic renewal, such as faith,
emotions, sexuality. Father Benedict brings the reader a
modern psychological approach tempered by common sense
and personal experience.

In the later chapters of the book, Father Benedict looks at
the clergy and religious life. His clinical assessment of religious life may at times sound harsh, but at the same time he
is hopeful that religious life can experience a rebirth. It is
clear from Church history that Francis, with his reform of
religious life, or Teresa of Avila and John of the Cross with
their reform of the Carmelite family, had a great impact on
the Church at large. Mother Teresa once stated that the
renewal of the Church depends on the renewal of priests;
however, we might add that the renewal of religious life
will help greatly the renewal of the Church. This renewal
begins with personal conversion, but it does not end there.
The asceticism and authority structure of religious life must
be rescued from modern tendencies toward individualism
and relativism. Society needs to find the careful balance
between personal freedom and responsibility to the common good.

American culture exalts individual freedom over most
other values. Truth, even life itself, are jeopardized by this
cultural bias that is so pervasive in our country. Reform will
require a common vision and commitment strong enough

to break through the patterns of secular society which are so ingrained in the American mind. Father Benedict faces these issues in his reflections on religious life in the United States.

Father Benedict is not "the subtle doctor". He is like John Hancock who wrote big so that King George would be able to see his signature without using his eyeglasses. For so long, people have denied the proportions of the crisis in religious life and the Church. Father Benedict looks for an explanation of the collapse of so many religious communities. Not everyone will agree with his conclusions, but I believe that his book will challenge all of us to confront the present realities and commit ourselves to work for a new flourishing of religious life and practice in the Church.

For the author, the topic of reform is not an academic one but rather part of a personal passion and spiritual odyssey which has led him to participate in the founding of a new community of Franciscans in the Capuchin tradition. The new family of friars will undoubtedly seem like a testing ground for many of Father Benedict's convictions. As we wait to see the results of this experiment, we ponder the eloquent cry for reform whose echo grows louder and louder.

†Most Reverend Sean O'Malley, O.F.M., Cap.
Bishop of the Virgin Islands

ACKNOWLEDGMENTS

I am deeply grateful to the great reformers of the Church who inspired this attempt to confront our times with this perennial message of the Gospel. I wish to thank Mother Claudia, I.H.M., for the title of this book and Fr. Joseph Fessio S.J. of Ignatius Press for his constant encouragement.

Preparing the manuscript would have been impossible without the very professional help of Charles Prendergast and Claudia McDonnell. I am grateful to Elaine Barone and Catherine Murphy, who type so very many things for me—and to John Lynch for the third magnificent cover he has provided for my books.

I am grateful, also, to my confrere and friend Most Rev. Sean O'Malley, O.F.M., Cap., Bishop of St. Thomas in the Virgin Islands for the Foreword, and to Richard Roach, S.J. of Marquette University for many suggestions.

Finally, I am grateful to the earnest young reformers of the Community of Franciscan Friars of the Renewal and the Community of Franciscan Sisters of the Renewal for the inspiration they have given me to hope that reform is possible in our time.

Fr. Benedict Joseph Groeschel, C.F.R.
Easter, 1990

Chapter One

REFORM: A HUMAN NECESSITY

Reform: A New Face

Religion is dying or dead. This is the verdict passed by many in the Western industrialized nations, especially in northern Europe, where active participation in the churches is less than 10 percent. In the progressive countries of Scandinavia active participation is reduced to about 1 or 2 percent of the population. There are signs that this fatal illness is spreading to southern Europe, the United States and Canada, where active participation in Church life has dropped at least 50 percent since 1959.[1] Many of the large mainstream denominations count their losses in hundreds of thousands. The Catholic Church tends to retain people in membership long after any real participation has ceased, but it is safe to say that Mass attendance by Catholics has dropped at least 50 percent in the past thirty years. Religious communities and diocesan clergy continue to attract fewer and fewer members.

Is there a way out? This book proposes that the only effective way back to life is through the essential step described in the Gospel and indicated by all religions of the world. This reform focuses on individual spiritual development

---

[1] Will Herberg, *Protestant, Catholic, Jew: An Essay in American Religious Sociology* (Chicago: University of Chicago Press, 1983).

and thorough, ongoing personal reform, which then give rise to communal and societal reform.

An Unlikely Model

For most people the word *reform* conjures up a grim and unappealing specter. It wears an inky black cape of sorrow and has an angry face and an inhumane spirit. To dispel this image I have dedicated this book to one of the great reformers of Church history, Saint Clare of Assisi (1194–1253). Her bright, smiling, youthful spirit is captured by the painting on the cover of this book.

Clare did not start out to be a reformer but intended to respond to the call to love God and give herself personally to Christ. The same call had been received by Saint Francis. Clare was young and vibrant at a moment in history when the Church had grown old but was on the verge of the Fourth Lateran Council, a council of renewal. She and her sisters became part of the renewal called by Pope Innocent III, although I suspect that she was not thinking in these terms when she became the first sister of a new movement in religious life, which was called the *minori,* or little ones. Near her home there were many convents of cloistered Benedictine nuns who devoutly lived a life similar to that of pious aristocrats. She embraced a life of extreme poverty, humility and penance. This was the beginning of a reform movement that would affect large numbers of believers and change the face of Europe in the second half of the Middle Ages. Regis Armstrong, a distinguished Franciscan scholar, has written that Clare accepted the charism of Francis, expressed it in her own unique feminine way and, at a period of medieval history in which the role of women was also undergoing change, shattered many of the religious stereotypes.[2] Yet Clare was one of us. She did not have the extraordinary experiences of her guide, Francis. Quite likely she would never have become known throughout the world except for her relationship with this man, whom many consider the most popular Catholic saint. She said Yes to his call for reform and contributed aspects of her own personal being, which became essential elements not only of the Franciscan message but also of the entire reform movement and revitalization of the Church in the middle of the thirteenth century.

Clare changed religious life for women and made it possible for simple, ordinary souls, not merely for members of the aristocracy. Along with Francis, Dominic and their disciples, she opened the way for an increasingly vast number of ordinary people to enter the mainstream of Church life. She, more than any other woman of her time, epitomized the tender love and the burning personal commitment and desire to follow Christ that were the essence of medieval piety. She was a reformer par excellence, although she probably never thought of herself as one at all. As Armstrong says so well, "During the twenty-seven years between the death of Francis and her own, she is the living witness that strongly shapes the consciousness of the Franciscan family, and, during that period, unwittingly becomes a creative innovator of the religious life in the Church."[3]

We live in times that desperately need reform and spiritual renewal. I believe that this call to the revitalization prompted by divine grace is beginning to grow. I find it

[2] Regis Armstrong, O.F.M.Cap., *Clare of Assisi, Early Documents* (New York: Paulist Press, 1988), 9–30.

[3] Armstrong, *Clare of Assisi,* 10.

eagerly accepted by a growing number of young Christian adults. In the readjustments being made in response to the new role of women there are much bitterness and pain, but not so much among very young women. They missed the conflicts of the immediate past. They were too young. They are disquieted, even discouraged, by the current trends in Church life, which to them are dated and hackneyed. For them the sixties or even the seventies are far in the past. They look forward to the third millennium. Despite all the difficulties of our time they have the freshness and vitality of youth, although they bear the scars of a period of difficult transition. Like Saint Clare they are surprised and fascinated by something new and vital, the call of grace, the call to conversion and reform.

If you are interested in a new movement for the Church, a new start, a step away from deadly controversy, from endless meetings that go nowhere, from denial and pretense, then you may be interested in the possibility of the reform of renewal. The renewal of the Church brought about by Vatican II has grown old despite all the good things it accomplished. If you are interested in the other step, keep before your eyes this youthful and beautiful face of the young woman touched by grace. It is Clare, but it is also a young woman of our time who posed for this picture. She is one of thousands of young people touched by grace who have felt a new call for reform.

The Unavoidable Conflict

Whenever we seriously acknowledge to ourselves or to others that God has called us to be something, we are bound to be thrown into conflict. It is helpful to realize that this conflict is utterly unavoidable. The history of any religion, which summons people to a spiritual life, must include an account of this conflict.

All serious religions attempt to deal with, reduce and solve this conflict. This pervasive conflict finds its origin in the difference between the finite and the infinite, the passing and the eternal, between what is dying and what lives in unchangeable light. Ultimately the conflict is between that which in its poverty seeks its own good and that infinite love that seeks to give itself away. As Pascal points out, the conscious awareness of this conflict constitutes the real nobility of the human race and our only real superiority over the rest of creation.[4] As far as we know, of all the creatures in the cosmos, man is the only one who seeks to live forever. In fact, he is the only material creature who can ever say or think the mysterious word *forever.*

Although each of the world's great religions has had its prophets and seers, it was only to Israel that God spoke as a person speaks to his friends. It was Abraham who knew the Infinite One not as a "being above all being" but as a person who spoke back. The God of Abraham calls, summons, demands, forgives, loves. Beginning with Abraham's experience, his journey, his terrible test on Mount Moriah with his son Isaac and from then on, those who have been taught in the faith of Abraham have lived in a continuing, deeply personal conflict. They have wrestled with God and, like Jacob, have often limped away from the battle. Those who follow Abraham have had their virtues reduced to ashes before their eyes, like Moses; their sins thrown into their faces by God's prophets, like David; they

---

[4] Blaise Pascal, *Pensées,* trans. A. J. Krailsheimer (London: Penguin Classics, 1966), 59ff.

have endured martyrdom like Jeremiah and the Maccabees. They have betrayed God and have been forgiven by His mercy, like Aaron and the priests when they had to drink the ashes of the golden calf. Any relationship with the living God always leads to tension, conflict and failure and then to repentance and reform. From repentance and reform, starting over again, comes a rebirth to holiness and renewal. To this day all the spiritual descendants of Abraham struggle continually with their own reform and renewal.

Because the Christian faith grows out of the religious experience of the Jewish people, it is to be expected that it is filled with the same conflict of time and eternity, of weakness and holiness, that characterized the sacred history of its parent religion. And this expectation is completely fulfilled. In only one human life do we find this tension between the finite and the infinite completely realized; between the temporal and the eternal, the power of evil to destroy and the power of good to love and save. This is in the life of Jesus of Nazareth. No one can look thoughtfully at a crucifix and fail to recognize the conflict. The unbeliever reading the life of Jesus must admit that it was His own goodness, compassion and truthfulness that brought Him to His death. The believer knows more than this. It is the faith of Christianity that this man, this child born on earth and buried in the earth, is the Infinite One, and All-Loving One, the One whom Abraham and Moses knew as someone knows a friend. And from the beginning to the end of life there is conflict. From Herod to Pilate, from the death of the Innocents to the cry of the Good Thief, it is a battle between the infinite mystery of good and the frightening mystery of evil. Although finite, evil is powerful enough to inflict the crucifixion on the Holy One. The response to this conflict on the part of the Christian is twofold. First one must have a hope in the ultimate victory of good, the infinite, the true, the beautiful. This hope is epitomized in the Resurrection and in the promise of the Second Coming and Judgment, which will right all the wrongs of the world.

Repentance and Reform: A Call Addressed to All

The second response is more individual and personal. This response is a constant struggle to choose the side of good in the conflict. It is, as Moses said, to choose life or death, a blessing or a curse (Dt 30:1). In all men there is an observable tendency to choose the finite, the limited, the selfish and turned in, the passing, the line of least resistance. This tendency is often so powerful that it draws us to the side of what perishes before our eyes. Our Lord Jesus Christ did not hesitate to warn His followers of this. He called them relentlessly to the process by which they could undo the effects of this persistent destructive tendency. The process is called repentance and reform.

We hope to make it inescapably clear in this book that repentance with reform is the essential psychological process of the Christian life. At the powerful opening of the New Testament the first public words of the Son of God are "the time has come and the reign of God is at hand. Repent and believe the good news" (Mk 1:15). The parables in which we hear the very voice of Christ are powerful challenges to give up the passing and to embrace the eternal, to turn to self-giving from self-centered preoccupation. The Sermon on the Mount is an uncompromising call to follow in the way of the Infinite, of the Holy. *Holiness* is simply a word for the ultimate mystery of God. *Holy,* from our point of view, represents one pole of the conflict between eternity and time. That Jesus is the uncompromising preacher of reform is acknowledged by both orthodox Christian scholars, such as Schnackenburg, Jeremias and others, and rationalists, such as Bultmann, who admits the same thing, as we shall see.

Reform in the Life of the Church

It should come as no surprise that constant repentance, the regretful acknowledgment of sin, is one of two essential components of the Christian life. It also is clear that reform, the positive effort to change and overcome our tendency toward evil, is the cutting edge of an integrated Christian life. Those who pretend that the community of followers of Christ is perfect have neglected to take into account this important fact of life. Christ never claimed that His followers would be perfect, that is, beyond repentance and reform. The vacillating fisherman whom Christ chose to be the leader of His community is a compelling example of this. The Gospels recount Peter's constant falls and temptations, and Tradition suggests that his wavering continued to the end of his life. Awareness of the need for reform is simply the reflection of the conflict between time and eternity, between the self-seeking and self-transcendental, that we spoke about in the opening paragraphs.

However predictable, the sins and inconsistencies of Christ's followers are still scandals. Sooner or later almost all of us, in large ways or small, contribute to this scandal. We fail in innumerable ways to choose the lasting and eternal side of the conflict. And even when we do not choose evil, we choose the good so halfheartedly and with so many qualifications that mediocrity becomes our canon-ized status quo. Ultimately the choice is made by the indi-vidual in his own life. The choice for the halfhearted, the mediocre, is made with a good bit of naïveté and innocence by the majority of what are called ordinary people. In the Gospel Christ's attitude is one of pity toward this neglected multitude. But the Savior is much more demanding of those who would be His disciples. He makes absolute demands based on the conflict between good and evil, a conflict that He teaches will be resolved only at the end of the ages at the Last Judgment.

Those who answer the call to be disciples of Christ must face the uncomfortable fact that he who is not with Christ is against Him; he who does not gather with Him scatters. From the opening call to repentance through the Sermon on the Mount and on to the final prayer in Saint John, the Gospel is a book about repentance and reform.

One of the most pressing questions in Church history has been how to keep alive the vital spirit of reform in the Gospels. This is no small task. It is true that during the Roman persecutions and in times of oppression and distur-bance since then, reform has not been too great a problem. Persecution, with its trials and dangers, has galvanized the sincere followers of Christ into fervent prayer and brave deeds so that the choice between the passing and the eternal has been clearly defined. Turbulent and depressed times, wars and the recovery periods after wars, have generally turned the minds and hearts of most people toward eternity. The deep religious faith of oppressed ethnic minorities—for example, the Irish, the Poles or the black people in America during and after slavery—gives ample evidence of this fre-quently overlooked fact of religious history. But easier times, when earthly rewards are abundant and unexpected pleasures of life become available, often have the effect of obscuring the basic conflict. Christ's disciples find themselves less motivated to see life as the way of the Cross.

That people forget the conflict between time and eternity is an astonishing fact in light of the universality of death. Even in the best of times all suffer and die. But they forget their mortality between joys and sorrows. Although it is the task of the Christian community to keep eternity before the eyes of all and to point the way to the only adequate resolution of the conflict, all too often Christians themselves become involved in the confusion and may cause some of it.

When worldliness reaches into the heart of the Christian community, the bell of reform begins to ring again almost automatically. The call for reform will come from many quarters. It often begins as a popular outcry against the obvious hypocrisy of some ecclesiastics. The outcry also is often directed against civil government, which easily corrupts as the values of men become worldly and materialistic. Often it is the young and the elderly who see the need for reform, because youth is idealistic and old age may recall better times.

Religious leaders often become the voice of reform. Some of them are saintly people, and some are concerned and terrified by the course they see the world taking. Many reformers were saints, but many others were not. Some were wise, and some were foolish. It has been observed that if God relied only on the saints and the wise, He would not get much done, because there are very few of them. In recalling the followers of Christ to their responsibilities in this conflict, God uses poor sinners and fools. They do not accomplish as much as the saints and the wise, but there are a lot more of them to do the work.

At every moment in the life of the Church there are reformers calling Christians to return again to the Gospel. This is because repentance and reform are ultimately individual and personal obligations, which confront all believers, as we have seen. But it is only the saints along with those who are willing to listen to them who hear the call to a more sincere and total obedience to the Gospel. The impact on millions of admirers of the autobiography of the young French Carmelite Thérèse of Lisieux is evidence of this call. Thérèse as a child had caught the fire and absolutism of the Gospel.[5] Awareness of the conflict between time and eternity was the motivating force in the life of this young woman. It still has immense power to inspire us today.

We Live in a Time When Reform Is Needed

During the past twenty-five years, which have been a period of relative economic prosperity and upward mobility for most members of the Church in the Western countries, there has been a gradual loss of the sense of reform and repentance. This has come about partly because of the declining awareness of the conflict between time and eternity, between earthly contentment and eternal happiness. This decline is so enormous that for a Christian writer to suggest that we are choosing the wrong side of the conflict or that a conflict exists is practically scandalous. To question whether our values are too humanistic is to suggest that we have lost a prophetic element in our Christianity. To raise an outcry

[5] John Clarke, O.C.D., trans., *The Story of a Soul,* (Washington, D.C.: Institute of Carmelite Studies, 1976). See chap. 4.

against the worldliness and moral flabbiness of contemporary Christians is to risk being dismissed out of hand. To
announce a call for reform at this apparently halcyon moment
is to risk being accused of spoiling the fun. Since the old
propensity for rationalizing and intellectualizing our faults
is particularly strong among educated people, they can
dismiss the need for reform in anger, annoyance or semi-
amusement. But that does not remove the need for reform—
either personal or ecclesiastical.

In the following pages, the call for reform will be ex-
plored primarily as a Christian responsibility, namely, as
something that you and I need to pursue if we are to
take the Gospel warnings seriously. Reform is part of the
life of the Church. We will apply it to the Church as we
know her in the present time. It is useless to dig up the past
to justify the present, as if recalling the foibles of the
immediate past would justify our present misdeeds. It might
be helpful to remember that societies also need reform.
Social justice, not the inner call of grace, is the motive of
societal reform, but the two are entwined. At times we will
allude to the need for reform in the governments of nations,
especially in our own. The fact that in the United States
during these affluent times there are large numbers of
people living in economic misery suggests that reform is
needed in the life of our country. America and the rest
of the modern world need reform, but it will only begin
with individuals.

The following chapters explore the need for reform in
various aspects of life. Chapters One through Seven refer
to aspects of Christian life that are the concern of all
believers, such as faith, emotions, sexuality. Chapters Eight
and Nine are of special interest to only some of our readers,
namely, those interested in the reform of the clergy and

of religious life. These chapters can be read selectively. Chapter Ten, concerning reform in society, should be read by all. The Epilogue, describing steps toward a movement of reform, should be read as an integral part of the entire book.

Chapter Two

THE REIGN OF GOD TODAY

A Call That Never Ends

The account of the public life of Our Lord Jesus Christ in the Gospel of Saint Mark begins with words that ring out like the opening lines of a great symphony. They are restated throughout the New Testament like a powerful musical theme: "The time has come and the reign of God is at hand. Repent and believe the Good News" (Mk 1:15). Our Lord's words summarize so much of His teaching and are so essential to leading a genuine Christian life that anyone seeking to be an authentic follower of Christ must frequently review His words by meditation, study and prayer if the spiritual life is to come to fruition. In addition to the individual, communities in the Church, societies that consider themselves Christian and the whole Church herself must constantly repent and believe again with new fervor the Good News of salvation brought and proclaimed by Our Lord Jesus Christ.

In order for any renewal or reform to be well founded, it must be built on these words. Those who are seriously interested in reform and renewal must ponder the significance of Our Lord's words about the reign of God. They must ponder His radical and personal demands on individuals and on societies within the Church. This book is an attempt to appreciate the vital significance of the reign of God in our time.

We will begin our consideration by examining the moral teachings of Our Lord and of the New Testament writers as these are reflected in the belief and experience of the early Church. In our study we will be guided by the experience of the living Christian community during the two millennia in which the followers of Christ developed moral teachings and theological systems that reflected and applied the original teachings of the Master.

We will reaffirm a much forgotten truth, namely, the importance of ethical convictions and moral living for believers. But what is far more essential is that we *renew* our daily conversion, our daily ongoing repentance by the power of God's living word and the help of the gifts of the Holy Spirit. As we have already seen, repentance and conversion are not a single decision, a single act, but rather the work of a lifetime.

The Historical Context

Before we begin our study it is important to put Christ's call to repentance into a historical context. The words of Jesus "repent and believe the Good News" were first proclaimed to a little group of fishermen and farmers, with their wives and children, on the shores of the Sea of Galilee. These mysterious and powerful words shook some of those who listened to them and changed the course of their lives. Eventually these words undid the power and entrenched assumptions of the very civilization in which these people lived. The words of Jesus Christ called forth from the Jews and Gentiles who were capable of responding to them a new way of life, which was purified by three hundred years of bloody persecution and became the foundation of Western civilization.

But in every period of that two-thousand-year history the same process has had to go on. Again and again—in the Dark Ages, in medieval times, in the Renaissance, in the age of reform, in the Industrial Revolution, in our own century— these words were received by some and rejected by others: "Repent and believe the Good News." Those who attended the Second Vatican Council and formulated its decrees and those who responded to them with sincerity and intelligence were all answering the call: "Repent and believe the Good News."

Our Moment of History

We live in a conflictual and difficult moment of history. The initial reaction to Vatican II and to the complex and contradictory trends that accompanied it has come to an end. The Synod that marked the twentieth anniversary of the Council was a milestone indicating the end of the period of initial impact. The Synod members suggested that the past twenty years of Church history (1 percent of its total history) had been a collection of mixed blessings. Gerald Arbuckle, a priest and anthropologist, has summed up the postconciliar situation very well by pointing out that the Church is facing a unique challenge caused by the cultural upheaval in the West, the refusal of the secular world to respond to the call of Vatican II and the need for new pastoral approaches to evangelization. His analysis of the situation, although addressed to religious, needs to be seriously considered if one is going to understand the need for reform at the present time.[1]

With Vatican II, the Church firmly committed itself to an evangelizing partnership with the world. To our dismay, we discover that the world expresses minimal interest in our message. It is ostensibly self-sufficient, but harboring fears of a nuclear holocaust. It is a world divided into the haves and the have-nots, both within and between nations. It is a unique challenge, the like of which the Church has not faced since it opened itself to the Gentile peoples. Old clichés no longer work. New approaches are necessary. It is a world that demands of us evangelical and pastoral creativity. Unfortunately we religious who exist to be innovative specialists within the Church seem to have lost our nerve, exhausted from the widespread fall-out of the past twenty chaotic years. Without doubt we are experiencing the chaos, but sadly we miss its meaning. . . .

We cannot abstract in fact from the reality that the movement to shake Catholics into becoming pastorally aware of the world beyond their ghetto also coincided with a world in "unnatural" turmoil, a world of intense and countercultural liminality. The combined effects of the theological and cultural changes of Vatican II and the cultural revolution left Catholics breathless, lost in what seemed to be an ever increasing malaise, a loss of direction. People felt stunned, rootless, benumbed, never sure what was to happen next within the Church that for centuries seemed unchanging. They became exposed to movements and pressures they could not understand. The mass of intricate cultural supports that had protected the ghetto church for over a hundred years were suddenly removed. In the midst of the

---

[1] Gerald Arbuckle, *Strategies for Growth in Religious Life* (New York: Alba House, 1986), xv.

confusion and disarray, the Church seemed, for the first time in centuries, to be an uncertain trumpet.[2]

In such a time of confusion Our Lord's call to repentance must be embraced by every sincere Christian—liberal, conservative or middle-of-the-roader—in the context of our present historical moment. But it would be silly to respond to Christ's calls to reform as if it were 1950 or 1865. We must respond to them as they affect us individually in the present context of our lives. The words of Jesus are a personal call. The Gospels are not simply classical literature containing a perennial meaning like the words of Dante or Shakespeare. The word of God is not merely a classic. For this reason, to read the Bible and especially the New Testament as a part of great literature is to miss the whole point of Christian faith. The words of Jesus are the words of a living person. By a mysterious power they are addressed to every moment of time. To you and me living in this moment they are a call to repentance and reform.

We live in a time of profound confusion, both for society and for the Church. There is universal confusion about how man is going to use the technological developments made possible by nuclear energy and computer science. There is the political confusion in the East and West and in the Third World arising from pressing questions about fulfilling human needs in a rapidly growing population with all its demands. The fact that this growing population is becoming constantly more educated and being stimulated by communication to want even more of this world's goods creates conflicts that become ever more dangerous. The haves and the have-nots and the great group of people in the middle are all stimulated by a practical materialism that can

[2] Arbuckle, *Strategies,* 13.

undermine both faith and human dignity. Parents in this age of confusion can attest that giving everyone in the family a television and an automobile generally does not lead to harmony and personal development.

The Conflict among Believers

You and I are well aware of the religious dimension of life. We are all the more concerned that in the confusion of our times values expressive of the human dignity of the children of God be respected. We care deeply that the good, true and beautiful things about man will survive. As believers we see that the repository of these values is Judeo-Christian Tradition, which speaks to us not only through the Church we belong to but also through the wider community of believers in God. And we the members of this worldwide collection of believers are likely to be frightened and frequently in deep conflict with one another about possible solutions. We are frightened by things like the proliferation of nuclear weapons as well as the animalistic and sadomasochistic stimulation in the media. We are appalled by the collapse of family life and marriage. Yet members of religious groups in the United States are themselves deeply divided over such issues as the morality of extramarital sexuality, over the moral acceptance of homosexual acts and especially over abortion. If the unity of religious believers that emerged in the ecumenical movement meant anything at all, it is now being eroded and destroyed by these present conflicts.

The Conflict in the Church

But there is a much more painful conflict beyond all this, and that is the conflict within the Catholic Church herself. It is no consolation that equally painful conflicts exist in the major Christian denominations and in the Jewish community as well. However, because the Catholic Church is a single structure, the conflict appears to be more intense. In the Catholic Church the opposing sides cannot simply walk away from each other. The present conflict in the Church often bothers us most because of what are really less important reasons. For instance, we are distressed because conflict creates a bad impression, especially when the media latch onto it and sensationalize it on television. The conflict is embarrassing, since it leads to moral confusion. It can cause scandal, which then leads to loss of faith in the Church and in her Creed. The intellectual content of faith, the saving knowledge of Our Lord Jesus Christ, as Saint Paul calls it, is muddled by poor teaching, theological dispute and the dilution of religious doctrine by superficial and trendy notions gathered from psychology and sociology—however useful these sciences may be when seriously applied.

It is astonishing how little knowledge of the fundamentals of faith and Catholic teaching sincere young people have when they knock on a seminary or convent door today. And these are the green wood. What must go on with the dry wood—those who have little or no exposure to the teachings of faith?

While the battle between what are styled as traditional Catholics and liberal Catholics goes on apace, actual participation in the works of the Christian life, such as the observance of the Commandments and the Sermon on the Mount, actually diminish. On average, many suspect that those who consider themselves good Catholics—clergy, religious and laity—spend less time and energy on prayer, meditation and religious studies and on works of charity and justice than good Catholics did before the Vatican Council. There are many exceptions, of course. There are new emphases, like dedication to the care of the poor, and not by just a few missionary-minded souls. There are many new engaging forms of religious experience. But when all is said and done, I do not think anyone can deny that there is an overall decline in committed practice of the Christian life by American Catholics. The decline in numbers of clergy and religious engaged in education, medical care and charitable activities is appalling. Thank God there are exceptions, but these exceptions usually reflect the personally expressed commitment of individuals rather than of whole groups or communities.

A Call Given Again

I am not here to bury the Church, the clergy, religious or anyone else. I am writing in order to identify and encourage a new voice that can be heard faintly in the Church. It is a newly given summons, which I first read in the writings of Pope John Paul II and specifically in his first letter to priests and bishops. He called priests to personal daily examination of conscience and to frequent acts of repentance and change. The Pope wrote to the clergy in the first year of his pontificate: "Being converted means continually giving an account" before the Lord of our hearts about our service, our zeal, our fidelity . . . of our negligences and sins, of our timidity, our lack of faith and hope, of our thinking only "in a human way" and not "in a divine way".[3] It is a call that could guide us during this time filled with conflict, and perhaps it could even lead us out of it: "Repent and believe the Good News."

The Call in the New Testament

In order to give a full and valid interpretation of these most important words, I have relied on the scholarship of the eminent biblical scholar Father Rudolf Schnackenburg and his classic work *The Moral Teaching of the New Testament*.[4] In 1962 Schnackenburg published this exploration of the biblical foundations of the Church's moral theology. He was rightly convinced that in this age of new ideas it would be essential for scholars and other informed Christians to have a firm grasp of the moral teaching of Our Lord and of the New Testament writers, especially Paul, John and James. As I studied the beginnings of Christian moral theology, it struck me that it would do many Catholic thinkers a great deal of good to go back to the foundations of Christian morality. These foundations go far beyond any dimension of philosophical ethics and even beyond the Old Testament moral teachings, although neither of these is denied. Christians apparently tend to forget that Jesus Christ clearly indicated that His moral teaching, as Saint Paul clearly reiterates, went beyond the demands of what had been given in the Law.

[3] Pope John Paul II, *Letter to Bishops and Priests of the Church,* April 9, 1979 (Boston: St. Paul Books and Media, 1979).
[4] Rudolf Schnackenburg, *The Moral Teaching of the New Testament,* 3d edition (London: Burns and Oates, 1982).

What Is the First Moral Demand of Jesus Christ?

The first requirement Jesus Christ put on all those who would follow Him is not obviously a moral or ethical imperative. It is simpler and more fundamental than all morality. It is the deliberate choosing (often the desperate choice) of Jesus of Nazareth as one's Savior and Redeemer, as the Son of God Who makes us God's adopted children, so that we may be saved from perdition and brought to eternal life. "Save us, Lord: We are perishing" (Mt 8:25), the words of the apostles in the sea, sum up this decision. One must experience this impulse in the depths of one's being, like a drowning man who grasps for a floating object in the waves. We are perishing, and we must be saved. Without this grasping of the Good News, Christian morality and Christian life itself do not effectively exist. And since we vacillate, forget, slip backward and sideways, as we learn from the apostles themselves, we must often renew our acceptance of salvation and grace from Jesus Christ by apparently starting all over again. I say apparently because in one obvious sense once we have accepted Christ as our Savior, we are adopted by God as His children. He does not reject us, but we can reject Him, partially or entirely. We can lose our grasp on our Savior in many ways—some apparent, some real. For instance, we can lose Him psychologically by disturbance and depression; ideologically by error, confusion and doubt; morally by sinful desires and behavior. In the case of truly mortal sin this loss is existential and complete. It can deprive us of our eternal salvation, which Christ won for us on the Cross. It is my experience that many times our loss of Christ as Savior is only apparent, even though it may cause great grief. Think of the experience of Joseph and Mary seeking for the lost Christ Child in Jerusalem.

Whatever the reign of God may mean, however it may be defined, serious New Testament scholars agree that Jesus announced Himself as the one who brought this reign, which had been promised by the prophets of Israel. He chose to be a different kind of Messiah from what His contemporaries expected. Nevertheless, it is an intimate part of His announcement that the rule of God is at hand. After reviewing the various biblical sources and various opinions on this doctrine, Dr. Schnackenburg writes:

> Our conclusion must, therefore, be that for Jesus, his claim to be the Messias was closely connected with his declaration that the reign of God is at hand. In his person, in his words and deeds, the time of fulfilment had come. And yet it had not come exactly as the Old Testament had expected. The time of fulfilment was not yet the time of completion. In Jesus' preaching, the kingdom of God "in power and glory" is still a thing of the future. Does this not mean that the situation in the history of salvation was still the same as it had been in the time of the prophets? No, because in Jesus the Messias had come; because with the mandate and by the power of God he healed the sick, called sinners (Mark 2:15–17 par.), remitted sins (Mark 2:5–10 par.: Luke 7:36–50), because with divine authority he announced the truths of salvation and the will of God (Mark 1:22 par.), so that the "acceptable year of the Lord", the great and final time of salvation had dawned . . . and the coming of the kingdom of glory, become certain—as certain as the coming of harvest after sowing, or as the mighty tree follows from the grain of mustard seed buried in the ground (cf. the parables of growth in Mark 4 and Matthew 13). . . . It is both present and not yet present; it is present in the person of the Messias, his words and saving acts, but not yet present as the cosmic kingdom of peace and glory. There is, however, an intrinsic

connection, an irresistible dynamism, linking this beginning
and the end, between this "penultimate time" (as Cullmann
called it) and the ultimate accomplishment. The last act in
the drama of salvation has begun: God himself is bringing
his work to an end, despite all resistance of the Evil One.[5]

Thus the kingdom of God has come, but if I may use a
simple term, important phases of its fulfillment are still to
come. As a rabbi friend of mine said when we discussed
Jesus as Messiah, "What has changed?" Certainly all has not
changed. There are still sins, injustices, wars and natural
calamities. But what has changed is this, that the disciples of
Jesus are called to a new relationship with God, with each
other and with their fellowmen. They may not achieve this
relationship. They may not even recognize it and may act
worse than pagans. They may merit a far worse punishment
because they are called to a new concept of self and to
a new relationship with God and with others. But by the
Holy Spirit Whom Jesus sent they are enabled, however
imperfectly, to live up to this relationship.

Jesus' Fundamental Demand

But now we come to the most important aspect of the
acceptance of Jesus, and that is conversion and repentance.
Dr. Schnackenburg puts it more forcefully than I can:

> The fundamental, though not the ultimate, demand made
> by Jesus on those who wished to participate in the reign of
> God was that they should repent. The Greek word metanoia
> conveys a Hebrew and Aramaic concept that goes beyond
> the scope of the Greek meaning "change of mind" and

[5] Schnackenburg, *Moral Teaching,* 18–19.

"regret". To the Semitic mind it suggested a man turning away from his former path, now recognized as wrong, and striking out in a completely different direction. Conversion or repentance, therefore, is (a) the total attitude of a man, involving all his powers; (b) a religious action, a resolute total turning to God; (c) not merely a turning away from, and atonement for, sins committed (repentance and penance) but also a new orientation for the future; (d) quite often a conversion in belief, or at least a new and deeper understanding of God and his holy will; (e) finally, an answer to the call of God's grace, a grasping of the opportunity of salvation offered by him.

The goal of religious moral conversion is God. But even in this endeavour to cut oneself off from all one's sins and find one's way back to God it is easy to go astray, for example if the penitent loses his way among externals. To counter this danger, the prophets laid special emphasis on inward turning away from sin and innermost turning towards the holy God, rather than on such penitential practices as fasting, wearing penitential dress and making lamentations. "Rend your heart and not your garments" (Joel 2:13). Outward proofs of penance must follow the attitude of mind: the "fasting" which is pleasing to God involves freeing captives, breaking bread for the hungry, taking in the homeless and clothing the naked (Isa. 58:6f). Repentance must, therefore, be expressed in the whole conduct and especially in works of loving assistance.[6]

Most readers of this book will have read these paragraphs of Schnackenburg with only mild interest, because they seem so obvious and are almost trite. We accepted this need for inner conversion long ago, we say. But is that really true? On any journey, no matter how far one has traveled,

[6] Schnackenburg, *Moral Teaching,* 25–26.

it is possible to take the wrong direction, even to reverse oneself in an instant. The external trappings of a disciple—customs, participation in rituals, repeated slogans—may all create an illusion of discipleship that is no longer genuine or integral. Every disciple of Christ must be like the first disciples, prepared at all times for the need to repent, change and get back on course.

The Forgotten Element

There is another element in Jesus' teaching on conversion, and that is something that so many modern writers on morality and ethics seem to minimize or even ignore, namely, the reality of the Last Judgment.

Jesus announced the reign of God, but as we have seen, it has not come as completely as promised. We experience this imperfect coming in our own lives. Our moral behavior must be that of those who are awaiting the complete coming of the reign of God. As Saint Paul writes, we must be in the world but not of the world (1 Cor 7:31). This fact is at the very heart of the drama of Christian experience. There is the imperative expectation that God's children will accept His reign or face the terrifying frustration of their total existence.

This is very different from the various other more or less sincere ethical attitudes that Christians may accidentally absorb in our culture. Let us review these, since religious people may accidentally accept these positions thinking that they are the Christian teaching, which they are not. There is the position of natural or philosophical ethics. This is the moral attitude of the good person trying to decide how to live as a decent human being. One finds many people in this position in our secularized world. It is worthwhile and praiseworthy, as Saint Paul acknowledges in the Epistle to the Romans, but it is not the doctrine of salvation. It is acceptable for an unbeliever, but it is not what you and I are pledged to by baptism.

Then there is the moral life as reflected in the inspired words of God in the Hebrew Scriptures, especially in the Ten Commandments. In the New Testament this is called the *Law*. It is a divine call to a higher morality, but as Paul points out, it has no power to save; furthermore, it makes demands on fallen human nature that one cannot live up to.

Beyond the Law there is the moral life of the adopted child of God as Christ proclaimed it in the Gospel. His teaching assumes and subsumes all that is good in ethics as the mind can discover these things, and all that is in the Law of Moses. But it makes new and incredible demands, which arise from Jesus' unique image of God as a loving, compassionate and forgiving Father, Who nevertheless demands an ever growing commitment of love from His children.

Schnackenburg's powerful words on the urgency of Jesus' moral teaching can easily be related to the historical moment in which we live. Ours is perhaps a time when it is clearer than at other times that after Christ we live between the announcement of the reign of God and its ultimate conclusion. While the idea that one's behavior will have effects on one's destiny after this life is emphasized in the Law and is often even recognized in philosophical ethics, Jesus focuses on the ultimate outcome of the reign of God as a judgment leading to salvation in a way unique to His teachings.

> This tension between partial fulfilment and expectancy of the end, between present salvation and future salvation, provides a fertile source of moral obligation. . . . In his meta-

phorical language, Jesus lays down conditions for "entering the kingdom of God", not thereby implying that we earn it [it is given us only by the decision of God, and we can only pray for it (Matt. 6:10)], but rather in the sense that only those who now accept and follow the words of Jesus will one day hear him pronounce those other words, "Come, ye blessed of my Father, possess the kingdom prepared for you from the foundation of the world" (Matt. 25–34). . . .

It was Jesus' keen desire to make men alert, prepared and resolved to total devotion to God, so he showed himself as a prophetic and forcible preacher, rousing bemused human beings who, though able to interpret the sign of coming storms on land and in the skies, did not recognize the hour of salvation (Luke 12:56). . . . As those dwelling at Sodom went unconcernedly about their business until one day fire and brimstone rained down from heaven and annihilated them all, so it shall be in the final catastrophe before the coming of the Son of Man. It also seems to have been Jesus' purpose in many of the parables to point out to his hearers the seriousness of the situation, the crisis of the times, which made it imperative for them to come to a decision. Only a person who is converted and believes can participate in God's reign.[7]

Unless we acknowledge that the moral teachings of Jesus Christ are linked to the Last Judgment and the final destiny of each individual, we cannot really comprehend the reign of God. The missing element in much contemporary thinking, even of Christians, is the recognition that Jesus taught that our moral acts have eternal significance.

[7] Schnackenburg, *Moral Teaching,* 19–21.

What Is Conversion Like?

And so conversion is an essential and imperative part of
Jesus' teaching. The parable of the prodigal son gives a clear
account of Jesus' concept of conversion. It begins with an
awareness of utter destitution and the inability to survive
apart from the generosity of God. The prodigal son is
destitute, debased and dying of starvation. He has no right
to ask for his father's forgiveness or help, yet his father is full
of joy and enthusiasm to see his return. The father accepts
him without punishment and gives him signs of honor and
decoration. Almost as an afterthought Our Lord includes
the element of the reliable son, warning the disciples against
the most dangerous obstacles to real repentance on the part
of believers—self-righteousness and presumption. If you
have not given sufficient thought in your own life to the
complete destitution and helplessness of the person symbol-
ized by the prodigal son, you should review the twelve
steps of Alcoholics Anonymous. (For your convenience
they are included in Appendix One.) Many spiritual writers
rightly assume that the utter destitution that these steps
reflect is actually the spiritual state of all men.

We are called to repentance as followers of Christ not by
the natural law reflected in philosophical ethics or by the
Mosaic Law given in God's own word but by the reality of
God's love for us and call to us. Jesus requires that His
followers repent in such a way that they admit their
powerlessness over sin and their inability to save themselves.
The disciple must follow the highest expression of the
Mosaic Law and love God with all his heart and soul and
strength and his neighbor as himself for the love of God
(Mk 12:30). But this implies going beyond self, a very real
death of self and an ability to endure the suffering and pain

that the death of self continually causes. "If any man would come after me, let him deny himself and take up his cross and follow me" (Mt 16:24).

Do we die to ourselves once and for all? The answer is obviously no. Ask Peter. Ask Paul. Ask the apostles and saints of the early Church. Repentance as taught by the Gospel is the *via crucis,* the way of the Cross. This is required as long as the journey of life goes on. It makes Christian spirituality a journey and advance toward the highest form of human development in the face of the obstacles of a fallen human nature.

For this reason the New Testament writers—Peter, John, Paul and James—all see the Christian life as an ongoing conversion. They see it as continual repentance, a daily acknowledgment that one is unable to save oneself and a complete turning to God.

Unfortunately, when Christianity becomes too comfortable, when it gets bedded down in a kind of pious materialism, when it forgets the powerful confrontation that one finds when Jesus preaches the Good News, it loses its sense of ongoing repentance. Devout Christians may, at such a time, occupy themselves neurotically with picking out their little faults while the rest of Christianity, unmoved by the thought of repentance, blissfully accepts that everyone is saved, that we are all going to heaven in a toboggan and that there is no possibility of eternal loss. At such times, one can expect a severe decline in religious life and other institutions of the Church. Christianity is based on repentance and on the awareness that we must struggle to take hold of the kingdom of God in our daily lives. When Christianity does not do this, it begins to become anemic and may even die away in some parts of Christendom. This has happened many times in the history of the Church. Is it happening now?

Conversions: Renewal or Reform?

Consider the extreme confusion of our time and the scandal and discord in the Church. Consider the decline in piety and religious devotion. Recall that in our country the gap between rich and poor becomes wider every day, and the number of people falling into the underclass increases.[8] When we consider all of this, it is time to admit that we live in days that desperately need repentance. The word *renewal* has been used for the last twenty-five years. It is a good word. In the Pauline context it means to return to the power of the Holy Spirit and let Him make us new again (Rom 12:2). But before that renewal can occur, reform is necessary. True spiritual renewal is not simply cultural or educational. It is not simply restating truths to make them more compatible with a new age. True renewal is above all a return to God. It is a daily, ongoing repentance, an attempt to accept the Good News in all its unthinkable and incomprehensible grandeur and to pick oneself up and try to respond to that call. Renewal without reform is spiritually devastating.

---

[8] Cf. *Economic Justice for All.* (Washington, D.C.: National Conference of Catholic Bishops, 1986). "In March 1990 the National Center for Children in Poverty (an affiliate of the School of Public Health of Columbia University) released a report demonstrating that the number of children under six years old who live in poverty (in 1987 the "poverty line" was a yearly income of $11,600 for a family of four) rose to 23% from 17% in 1968. This report is available from the Center at 154 Haven Avenue, New York, NY 10032.

Where Does Reform Begin?

More and more Christians are saying that we have arrived
at a time for reform—even a reform of renewal. Where does
this reform begin?

It begins with individuals. Group efforts at reform often
lead to discord and even to religious war. They ignore the
first step. Individual repentance and reform must happen in
the life of every Christian who believes and listens to the
summons to repent and hear the Good News. This is the
hour for repentance and reform. What are we going to do
about it? Listen to what Saint Paul says about the relationship of renewal and reform:

> I appeal to you therefore, brethren, by the mercies of God,
> to present your bodies as a living sacrifice, holy and accept-
> able to God, which is your spiritual worship. Do not be
> conformed to this world but be transformed by the renewal
> of your mind, that you may prove what is the will of God,
> what is good and acceptable and perfect [Rom 12:1–3].

If we attempt renewal without repentance and personal
reform, it is not a work of God. It is at best an artistic
movement like the religious art of the Renaissance. If
we attempt reform without repentance, it becomes self-
righteousness and bitter zeal. If we attempt repentance
without the daily sustained recognition of our complete
dependence on God, we fail. Saint Augustine, who was a
strong force for renewal and reform in his time, recognized
this prayerfully in his *Confessions:*

> At the present time we move towards doing good, since our
> heart is so conceived by Your Spirit: but at an earlier time
> we moved towards doing ill, for we had gone away from
> You. But You, God, who alone are good, have never ceased

to do good. Some indeed of our works are good through Your grace, but they are not eternal: after them we hope we shall find rest in the greatness of Your sanctification. But You, the good, who need no other good beside, are ever in repose, because You are Your own repose.

What man will give another man the understanding of this, or what angel will give it to another angel, or what angel will give it to a man? Of You we must ask, in You we must seek, at You we must knock. Thus only shall we receive, thus shall we find, thus will it be opened to us.[9]

---

[9] Augustine, *Confessions,* trans. F. J. Sheed (London: Sheed and Ward, 1944), xiii, xxxviii.

Chapter Three

FIRST AND ONGOING CONVERSION

Most of my readers, I suspect, have never been through a great conversion, a total change of life with a complete uprooting of the past, indicating a totally new direction. Consequently, like most born Catholics, we have given little thought to what conversion is. When we have thought about it, we usually did so because some friend or relative was going through a conversion. Often enough new converts disturb us because of the freshness of their vision or the total sincerity of their practice of their newfound Faith. Or it may happen that someone, often an evangelical Protestant friend, comes along and says that we all need to be born again, converted anew, and that our lifelong attempt to be a follower of Christ is not enough.

If you are like me, this will cause you to pause and think, Did I miss something? I ask this question seriously, because I have been dissatisfied with my response to the call of the Gospel every day of my life since I received my First Communion.

A word must be said here about the growing number of young Catholics who actually did give up the practice of their Faith and later returned to it with a real personal conversion. (Usually they have dropped the practice of their Faith because it had been communicated in a confused and anemic way.) They are an encouraging breath of fresh air and may represent the most vibrant hope for the real reform of renewal.

It must be obvious that there are two modes of conversion. The first is a profound and sudden conversion; the second, the lifelong struggle to walk on the road of Christ, trying to carry the cross and, with painstaking effort, to make gradual progress. Both are found in Scripture and in the lives of the saints. In fact, the lives of the saints indicate that the startling, immediate first conversion is real only if it is followed up by the lifelong conversion. Two texts from the New Testament will illustrate this very pointedly:

> Suddenly, while he was traveling to Damascus, and just before he reached the city, there came a light from heaven all around him. He fell to the ground and heard a voice saying, "Saul, Saul! Why do you persecute me?" "Who are you, Lord?" he asked. "I am Jesus, and you are persecuting me. But get up and go into the city, where you will be told what you must do." The men traveling with Saul stood there speechless, although they heard the voice they could see no one. Saul got up from the ground, but even with his eyes wide open he could not see anything at all, and they had to lead him into Damascus by the hand [Acts 9:3–9].

Contrast this sudden conversion with the following writing by the same Saul of Tarsus, who is now Paul the Apostle:

> Not that I have become perfect yet; I have not yet won, but I am still running, trying to capture the prize for which Christ Jesus captured me. I can assure you of this, my brothers, I am far from thinking that I have already won. All I can say is that I forget the past and I strain ahead for what is still to come; I am racing for the finish, for the prize to what God calls me upward to receive in Christ Jesus. We

who are called perfect must all think this way. If there is some point of which you can see things differently, God will make it clear to you; meanwhile let us go forward on the road that has brought us to where we are [Phil 3:12–16].

These last words were written in 56 A.D., approximately twenty years after Saint Paul's conversion on the road to Damascus.

The latter text tells us much about ongoing conversion. It indicates that an ongoing conversion is not such a powerfully emotional event as the initial conversion. One could not possibly engage all the emotions and powers of the psyche in such a high level of attention and keep this sustained for a long period of time. Once in a while, we meet someone who keeps an emotional fervor at fever pitch, and we may observe one of two things. The person is either insane ill advised and likely to burn out or disturbed and suffering from such a high level of emotional disturbance that religion has become a vehicle for the expression of troubled emotions.

The dramatic first conversion, which may take place in an instant as it did with Saint Paul or over a period of time as it did with Saint Augustine and Saint Francis, is a special gift of God, an actual grace. Augustine describes it so well in the *Confessions:* "You shouted out, O Lord, and broke through my deafness. You burned brightly and chased away my blindness. You breathed your fragrance upon me and even now do I pant after you. You touched me and I burned for your peace" (book X, xxvii).

The first conversion is most dramatic when it happens in the life of an unbaptized person. But it can happen to a baptized person who has been a lukewarm Christian or to one who is a backslider, that is, one who no longer practices his religion. In the case of Saint Teresa of Avila, who was a worldly nun, or Saint Catherine of Genoa, who was a despondent member of the nobility, we have the example of a lukewarm Christian. There is also the example of Matt Talbot, a Dublin dock worker who was a severe alcoholic. Each of these people had some kind of religious practice. In the case of the first two, there appears to be at least a sincere, if lukewarm, adherence to the life of the Church. Most people would have considered Teresa and Catherine good Christians before their conversions, and without his conversion Matt Talbot would have at least received Church burial.

Certainly some of my readers are Catholics who have been reconverted long after baptism. They have been brought back to the Church by the grace of God from a rather mindless existence in which there was only superficial religious practice or affiliation.

If you are one of these converts, I suggest that you keep very much in mind the graces you received at your reconversion. Perhaps it would be helpful once in a while to write your conversion down and go over the graces you have received. Many converts and reconverts annually remember the day of their conversion and make a special effort to recall that day with prayers of thanksgiving and special good works of charity. The troubles of life and its apparently meaningless humdrum are very helpfully broken up by the remembrance of important spiritual events in life. Just as a person celebrates the anniversary of ordination or marriage, one can joyfully recall a return to God.

A word should be said about those who have reconverted once or twice and now are in need of conversion again. This phenomenon may be linked to a personality trait, or it may be the result of a lack of good spiritual guidance at the time of the first conversion. I have known people who have fallen away a couple of times, and then in later years have made their way back again. In the parable of the unclean spirit that returns with seven other spirits, Our Lord lets us know that conversions that are later abandoned can lead to very difficult situation. But with God all things are possible, and so the Lord Who calls us all can call again and again in His mercy.

Ongoing Conversion

What does ongoing conversion mean? How do we conduct ourselves to make it more productive? What do we do to move ourselves along, especially if we are in the doldrums? And, finally, what does ongoing conversion have to do with the confusing situation in which the Church now finds herself?

Ongoing conversion is ultimately the spiritual journey seen from the negative point of view. Spiritual development is the gradual growth of the individual toward complete union with God in eternal life. In this sense, the spiritual journey is a positive experience of growth. But spiritual development takes place in the face of tremendous obstacles: for instance, the effects of original sin, which are absolutely insurmountable without the unmerited gift of God called grace, which has been won for us by the life, death and resurrection of His Son. The effects of this mysterious primeval reality include the loss of everlasting life, the complete frustration of our purpose of existence, the darkening of the intelligence, the weakening of the will, the severe disturbance of the emotional life and physical incapacity and death in their present appalling forms.

Flowing from these effects are consequences that are

deeply disturbing to human relationships on a personal and societal level and that lead to crime, injustice and profound personal hurt inflicted even on those we love.

These damaging consequences in turn lead to war, murder and slavery in societies and deeply conflictual relations between families and friends. These are only some of the negative effects of the mysterious fall of the human race, which resulted from a violation of divine justice but led to the immensity of divine mercy shown in the Old Testament. The divine mercy is completely revealed in God's Son, whose life and death show how much God loved the world.

The struggle against all of these obstacles is what we call conversion or repentance, and its result is what we call reform, or putting things back into the shape in which they were supposed to be.

There is a psychological, and even physical, parallel to conversion, and this is healing or therapy. As people grow, they may encounter various pathological states that have been part of their adjustment since childhood or infancy. This fact is acknowledged by the majority of psychotherapists. We are becoming more aware of what is called preventive medicine. In most cases, preventive medicine is aimed not so much at preventing problems as at solving inborn deficiencies or coping with the effects of aging so that these problems do not get out of hand and cause more serious illness.

Much the same can be said of ongoing conversion. We are all subject to internal destructive forces called the seven capital sins. We all experience psychological malfunctions from infancy and childhood. Most of us have spiritually destructive traits, and we have developed spiritually damaging habits of mind and behavior. Ongoing conversion is the process of overcoming, healing or at least coping with these habits.

It is important to reaffirm here a fact that we modern people seem to ignore, namely, that the struggle against the forces of self-destruction and disintegration within us cannot be successfully carried out without the initial and continuing help of divine grace. Also, it cannot be completed without the special and extraordinary help of the seven gifts of the Holy Spirit. It is also the teaching of Saint Augustine, Saint Teresa and Saint Thomas Aquinas that we would never get started in this struggle unless God enticed us to do so almost against our will by a particular call of grace. As Saint Augustine says, "You were with me, but I was not with you."[1]

How does one conduct oneself in order to make ongoing conversion most effective? There are several steps, and these are summarized by Pope John Paul II in his letter to priests.[2] In this book I have borrowed extensively from the ideas of the present Holy Father.

Steps in Ongoing Conversion

I. *Gain Self-Awareness.* Any personality adjustment—and that is what ongoing conversion is in psychological terms— must begin with an awareness that something needs to change. People live in depression, misery, temptation, conflict and doubt for months and years and simply accept the painful situation as a necessary part of life. Or they blame it all on God and perhaps get angry at Him.

---

[1] Reginald Garrigou-Lagrange, O.P., *Christian Perfection and Contemplation* (St. Louis, Mo.: B. Herder, 1954), 107–13.
[2] Pope John Paul II, *Letter to Bishops and Priests of the Church,* April 9, 1979, (Boston: St. Paul Books and Media, 1979).

Sit down and ask yourself if you are really satisfied with the way you are responding to God's grace and Christ's call to discipleship. Are you responding as well as you might to other opportunities that life offers you? If you are satisfied with yourself, I suspect you are in real trouble. If you are not satisfied, then the next step is to ask what needs to be reformed. For example, a religious sister I spoke with could not pray because she was unaware of her immense anger. She was aware only of emotional pressure. When she faced her anger she was able to pray, although initially it was in an angry way. Deciding on what has to change is not easy. I have personally discovered that when one points out things that need to be changed in the Church or in communities, the following predictable defensive reactions may be expected:

— *Saying that everything is fine.* This is simple denial.
— *Saying that change is motivated by pride or some other vice.* In fact, we never do anything from pure motives. We always have mixed motives. We should try to purify them, but it does not mean that we refrain from acting until our motives are perfectly pure.
— *Fearing the consequences.* This is a very dangerous defense. Our Lord gave us the parable of the three servants with the talents to warn us not to be afraid of making a change, even though the consequences may be unpleasant (Mt 25:14–30).

2. *Plan a Strategy.* Change is difficult. You must develop a strategy for change, recognizing two distinct things. First you must realize that you get what you want over the long haul of life. If you want to do God's will but you also want something that is in conflict with that will, you have to resolve the conflict. If you do not, you are obviously going to remain in conflict.

Second, realize that you are really powerless to overcome serious spiritual obstacles, because the things that are opposed to your conversion are usually more immediately attractive. This is most obvious in the case of compulsive behavior, but it is the hidden fact in many other problems. We simply cannot heal ourselves. For this reason fervent intercessory prayer is necessary. We must constantly acknowledge that Jesus Christ is our Savior and that we do not save ourselves. Often we do not understand our own motives. We need to analyze the roots of our spiritual problems.

This is important because we can all blame someone else for our problems. People with spiritual problems may blame God, their parents, the Church, life or others, for example, a clergyman or some other person that they meet. Many times the roots of our spiritual problems are simply mishaps of a troubled world. Many people suffer from unresolved neurotic needs, that are the fault of no one in particular.

3. *Learn to Cope.* Make a list of effective steps for change in the order of their execution. For example, if you realize that your prayer life is dwindling away or is gone, set aside some particular time to pray and stay at it for a while. If you find that the time is unsuitable and you must change it, do so in an orderly way and still seek the same goals of improved prayer.

4. *Ensure That What You Are Doing Has a Solid Foundation.* You can do this by discussing your decisions with a friend. It is often helpful to check with a spiritual director or with someone else who is informed about theology. Do not try to do something that is impossible. For instance, a person who tried to reform himself by obliterating all temptation from life would be trying to do the impossible.

The Reform of the Church

These steps are the beginning of individual reform, but they are also the beginning of the Church's reform.

Long ago, in the troubled time right before the Reformation, Saint Catherine of Genoa made the point that the reform of the Church would begin only with individuals.[3] But this personal reform is the fruit of divine grace and must be shared with the Church. It is to be hoped that an awareness of reform and personal conversion may stop the dissipation of so much energy on the part of very good people who are seeking to grow in the spiritual life but are doing so in the wrong way. For twenty years an immense amount of energy has been wasted by clergy, religious and laity who have sought to grow spiritually without paying the price. They have attempted to do it by various psychological techniques and at times by things that could only be called cheap tricks by behavioral scientists.

There is no shortcut to holiness or to psychological maturity. If a person wishes to grow, the outline for reform is contained very clearly in the teachings of Our Lord Jesus Christ and in the examples of the saints who followed Him. There is no other way. Modern psychology—even pop psychology—may offer some insights and fresh perspectives that may be helpful. But these techniques are not capable of saving anyone. They cannot lead to genuine reform. You will achieve true reform and ultimately help reform the Church when you go into your room, close the door and pray to God in secret, not when you dissipate a great deal of energy, time and money on things that are fundamentally psychological gimmicks.

[3] S. Hughes and B. Groeschel, eds., *Catherine of Genoa* (New York: Paulist Press, 1979), 37–38.

Church reform will come when our attempts are solidly established on the rock of Jesus Christ as He is presented to us by the Scriptures and the Tradition of the Church and her dogmas and theological teaching. One thing that is not being tried in any particularly enthusiastic way by people who call themselves Catholics is Catholicism. If you go into a good library, you can find immense treasures of Catholic knowledge and truth, which have been preserved throughout the ages. In the 1940s and 1950s a group of distinguished scholars, many of them laymen, made the treasures of Catholicism available to Catholics. Scholars such as Gilson, Pégis, Maritain, Garrigou-Lagrange and Guardini collected and published great works of Catholicism in the years before the Council. It is time for us to get back to these classics so that reactions to the new insights of the Council may be theologically well grounded. Not long ago I visited a seminary where the librarian boasted that 90 percent of the library's books were only twelve to fifteen years old. It was not a library; it was a newsstand. At best it was a pocketbook gallery. A library is a treasury, a memory bank of human knowledge of many centuries. A Catholic library that is not such a treasury is a betrayal of a Church that claims to have a living Tradition down through the ages.

It seems to me that it is time to begin again intellectually, morally and spiritually. It is time to look at the foundations of Christianity and to compare them with the attempts in the past two decades to bring the Church up to date. None of these attempts should be accepted or rejected uncritically. Rather, a good Christian should try to be well informed on the changes. One of the serious obstacles to the reform of the Church at the present time, it seems to me, is theological and cultural ignorance. Not everyone can be expected to enter into an intellectual discussion of ecclesiastical change, but every person interested in the spiritual life has been given the intelligence necessary in his life. It is an observable fact that people normally have enough intelligence to deal with their environment. An intelligence wasted or left idle is clearly an obstacle to spiritual development.

Not only are we intellectually slothful, but also a great deal of moral shabbiness and confusion has entered into the lives of Christians of all denominations. This has given rise to dreadful public scandals. It has caused a decline in vocations, because so many young people are confused and disheartened by what they see. The road of moral conversion is the only way out for each of us.

We must ask ourselves if we have allowed our minds to become insensitive to untruth, to bad behavior, to immorality, to sexual confusion, to immodesty. These questions must be asked.

It takes a tremendous amount of personal dedication for a Christian to ask these questions and appropriately respond to them when very few people are taking them seriously. At this time it may be imperative to stand alone, even if this has never been necessary before. I once saw a sign that read, "Be honest. Don't bargain with your conscience. It's all you have." If we are not honest with ourselves and we pretend to be Christians—even clergy or religious—we have not only betrayed God. We have ultimately betrayed ourselves.

Reform Is Not Sad

There is nothing sad about a time of reform. Reform is fascinating, interesting, vital and energetic. Paradoxically, going along with the tide and floating along wherever things go can be very boring, dehumanizing and ultimately degrading to the individual. The Lord has given the perfect antidote to jaded and self-indulgent boredom: "Repent and believe the Good News."

I ask you and I demand of myself in this crucial moment in the history of civilization and of the Church that we repent, that we hear the Good News and embrace it and that we live by it so that nothing else is more important than that the kingdom of God be in our hearts and in the hearts of those around us.

One afternoon recently I happened to be at an impressive beatification ceremony in Saint Peter's Square. On the way out of the square I met Bishop Austin Vaughan of New York, and we fell into conversation on the problem of legalized abortion. He confided that he was coming to realize that he and, I might add, a good many of the rest of us had been too passive, too easy on this issue for a long time. He felt that we needed to make reparation to make up for our silence in the past. Since then Bishop Vaughan has been imprisoned a number of times for opposing abortion.

If we have to suffer misunderstanding and criticism for a strong prolife stand, which, after all, is the defense of help-less human beings, then we ought to recognize that these inconveniences and even indignities are a way of doing penance for our complacency and inconsistency in the past. This is one of the painful realizations of ongoing conversion. It must have come to Peter and the other apostles after they failed completely on Good Friday. This repentance and regret for past unwillingness to take a risk that is called for are the fuel of ongoing conversion.

Watch out! It is powerful fuel. It brought those same apostles to lives of total self-renunciation and to violent death. And it brought them to the glory of God in Christ Jesus Our Lord.

Chapter Four

THE CONVERSION OF THE MIND

Recently a priest friend recounted to me the following distressing incident. A brilliant young man from his parish took an exam in theology at a Catholic college. In completing the sentence "Jesus was _____", he inserted the word *divine.* The teacher, a priest, corrected this answer and put instead the word *unique.* During the course the teacher had consistently taken a position against the teaching of the Church enunciated in the Council of Nicaea (325 A.D.) in the condemnation of Arius and many times since.

Whatever distinction this teacher may have wished to make, there was no doubt in this student's mind that the divinity of Christ was being denied. It would appear that this teacher had missed one of the important steps of repentance—the conversion of the mind. Sadly, it is not unusual to find teachers in many churches who do not accept the fact that Christ called for a conversion of the mind, a going beyond the superficial significance of knowledge obtained by the senses. Christ is not alone among the great religious figures of history in calling men to go beyond materialism and skepticism. But He is alone, unique in this sense: He called those whom He encountered to believe that He was the Son of God. Before we can understand this conversion of the mind by faith, we need to consider what it is that the mind does.

The Function of Intelligence

Human intelligence is one of the greatest gifts of God. It reflects the divine attribute of total intelligence, or omniscience. Intelligence is fascinating to watch, especially as it develops in young children and as it comes to its neurological fullness in teenagers. I am among that group of stunned adults who stand by and watch the children of our decade deal efficiently with computers that leave me permanently befuddled.

Intelligence is a power that does several remarkable things. It reflects the reality of the world outside the mind, and it organizes this reality into categories, separating sky from land, cows from horses and even virtuous people from those who cannot be trusted. It also comes to conclusions and indicates effective steps to implement these conclusions. It tells us not only that the sky is overcast and that a storm may be coming but also that we should close the windows and doors. Intelligence tells us to put a saddle on a horse and put a cow in the pasture. It tells us to welcome a friend and to keep a careful eye on those we cannot trust. Intelligence is the key by which we deal with what we cannot perceive through the senses. Even the most primitive men used intelligence to deal with the invisible mysteries of life, perhaps by fashioning an idol or by magic, but nonetheless they tried.

And as man became more civilized, aspects of intelligence became more operative so that philosophy, theology and even mysticism and spirituality came into existence. These all represent very high functions of intelligence, enabling man to cope not only with storms but also with the idea of eternity. Intelligence supplies us with the knowledge not only of horses and cows but also of angels and God; not only of friends and foes but also of saints; it speaks of the Savior of the world as well as of those who would have been better off if they had had millstones hung around their necks.

Because of the observable fact that men can use the power of intelligence badly to lead themselves and others astray and even to destruction, intelligence must be integrated and at times governed by other factors. This is very important. Perhaps many modern people would not agree with such a statement, but I suspect that if you are reading this book, you would agree. For instance, the person who uses intelligence without regard to morality will sooner or later become a criminal before God and man. A shocking example of this lack of moral constraint in the use of intelligence can be seen in the behavior of Hitler's scientists, called "Nazi doctors" in a study by Robert J. Lifton.[1] They were brilliant men who, in the name of science, performed lethal experiments on innocent human beings.

Intelligence has to be guided by other considerations. It is limited in its expression by culture and by the exigencies of communication. When it comes to things too profound for a single human mind, intelligence must learn from what others have already deduced and go on from there. Human progress has occurred only because generations were willing to learn from the past, obviating the necessity of reinventing the wheel and rewriting the dictionary. In no place is this more obvious than in theology and science.

---

[1] Robert J. Lifton, *The Nazi Doctors* (San Francisco: Harper & Row, 1989).

Intelligence and the Things of God

Finally, when it comes to the things of God, human intelligence not only must be led by others but also must be picked up and carried beyond itself. While intelligence can come to some knowledge of an infinite creative force and even call this force God, it cannot, by its own ability, come to know the living and true God Who is a loving Father and Who sends His only Son into the world. Reason and intelligence cannot deduce this. Even when the mysteries of God are revealed, these transcendent realities seen by the eyes of the intellect are like the indescribable brightness of the transfigured Christ. Reason is overwhelmed. It must be led on in many ways. The intelligence must be informed, for example, that God is three Persons. It must be given comparisons or analogies to suggest realities with which it can deal—for example, the ideas that God is Father, that He is light and in Him there is no darkness. It must be given images and comparisons. For instance, we call Christ the Good Shepherd, and we are told that Christ is united with us as the head and members of the body are united. Intelligence must be given assistance so as not to go astray when using images and ideas, because all knowledge of what is revealed is like seeing "in a mirror darkly" (1 Cor 13:12).

We must constantly bear the limitations of intelligence in mind, lest we allow error or even heresy to find a home in our minds. Unless we use intelligence with great care and are willing to be guided by God's word and the Church, we will fall into error. For example, an analogy can be developed by the mind to such an extent that other revelations are minimalized in a disproportionate way. The brilliant theologian and reformer John Calvin wished to preserve the glory of God in the midst of Renaissance humanism, which had

become degenerate and un-Christian. He took some basically sound theological concepts (that glory is due to God
alone, that men cannot save themselves and that God knows
the future), and he developed a concept of predestination
that was so severe that he ultimately denied the Catholic
Faith in which he had been reared and educated. Calvin was
intelligent, prayerful, dedicated and sincere. But if you are a
Catholic, Orthodox Christian, Anglican, Methodist or
Baptist, even if you are a contemporary Presbyterian
or Congregationalist, you are likely to say that Calvin's
intelligence led him astray in this particular understanding
of God and his relationship to men. Four hundred years
later, in South Africa, a place of which Calvin never heard,
some Christians who are followers of the Calvinist tradition
are using his teaching to justify apartheid. I suspect that
Calvin would roundly denounce apartheid if he were alive
today. But our mistakes live on, especially theological
ones.

Another example closer to our time is Archbishop Mar-
cel Lefebvre, who was once the father general of a highly
respected religious community of dedicated missionaries.
He disagreed vehemently with many of the changes after
Vatican II, and as a result of taking certain excerpts of papal
documents out of context, he has in fact created his own
church, contrary to the law of the very Church he seeks to
defend. Like Calvin, he is a person of sincere faith and
devout life. And like Calvin, he is confused by some of the
limited concepts we have of divine revelation. Both men
have made—at least to my way of thinking—a fatal error.
They failed to accept fully that special gift from God that is
the guidance of the living Church. Saint Augustine and
Saint Thomas Aquinas teach something that is rather obvious when you think about it: all that we know about divine

reality we know through analogies, comparisons of things essentially dissimilar but accidentally similar.[2]

For this reason every intelligent person seeking God needs to be guided by the community founded by Christ Himself, the Church. Paradoxically, neither Calvin nor Lefebvre ever actually denied this. They both required their followers to accept the authority of the fragment of the Church they had gathered around themselves, but unfortunately they both ended up outside the living historical reality of the Church that Christ had founded.

Is there a danger that this may happen to any of us or to others who may have views very different from those of Archbishop Lefebvre?

Sadly, my answer is that it is happening on many sides and that we desperately need a reform of faith in the Catholic Church right now. Without such reform large numbers of people will continue to be drawn further and further away from the Catholic Faith and never even realize that they are drifting. Is a lack of the reform of faith the problem of the teacher mentioned in the opening of this chapter? I was appalled recently when crowds in Ireland flocked to hear an American priest presenting teachings that come very close to denying the Catholic doctrines of original sin, redemption and salvation and encouraging pseudoliturgical practices that include elements of paganism euphemistically

---

[2] Augustine, *De Trinitate,* VII, 4, 7. Aquinas, *Summa Theologica,* I, q. 12. Many modern theologians discuss this question of the natural knowledge of God and of ways of coping with revelation. The interested reader may find the following helpful: K. Rahner, *Foundations of the Christian Faith* (New York: Seabury-Crossroad, 1978), 44–89; H. U. von Balthasar, *Elucidations* (London: SPCK, 1971), 18–34; K. Wojtyla, *Faith According to St. John of the Cross* (San Francisco: Ignatius Press, 1985).

called natural religion or witchcraft. How did the people from the Isle of Saints and Scholars become intrigued by such original nonsense? They at least implicitly ignored or rejected a significant part of the Catholic theological Tradition while responding to their own impulses or needs. They may in fact have had some legitimate questions, as did Calvin and Lefebvre, but they were choosing to find the answer outside the intellectual framework of their own Creed and theology. This, tragically, is not an isolated case.

The Gospel Call to Faith

The only effective solution to the problem of personal insight versus faith is to return to the foundations of our Faith in the New Testament. Again Dr. Schnackenburg will be our guide as we take up the question posed by the false teaching mentioned at the opening of this chapter.

Christ called His hearers to repentance, but He also called them to faith. And that call is as absolute in the Scriptures and in the Church as it was the day Christ called out, "Repent and believe the Good News." In the following powerful passage Dr. Schnackenburg sums up the requirement of knowing and believing:

> The demand for faith is very closely connected with the call to repentance. Just as repentance is expressed outwardly by accepting Jesus and his messengers, so too faith is impossible without the adoption of an attitude of mind which itself is, in the wide sense, a "conversion", a complete turning towards God, a listening to his will, and obedience. The obduracy of the Pharisees and Scribes who did not follow John the Baptist was both unreadiness to repent and the lack of faith (Luke 7:29ff.; Matt. 21:32). Faith is, as it were, the positive side of conversion. "Believe in the Gospel" (Mark 1:15)

means, believe in the message about the kingdom of God
that Jesus brings, not in a cold, uncommitted way, but by
accepting in a positive fashion everything it involves for
each human being personally. The man who is convinced
that God is actively establishing his royal rule is bound
above all to strive for his part to fulfil God's royal will. And
if God announces his will through Jesus of Nazareth and
guarantees his identity by healings and miracles, then one
must accept and obey Jesus' words. Consequently faith, like
repentance, is a "total" attitude, claiming all man's faculties.[3]

This call to believe as a moral responsibility was not
something new. The children of Abraham were called, as
was that very man whom we call our father in faith, to
believe in the Lord, to assent intelligently to His words and
directives and to divorce themselves from the paganism
that surrounded them. But Abraham's faith and trust led
him beyond intellectual assent to a mysterious God, a
God more puzzling than the idols of the pagans. Abraham
and his children were called to a whole life of faith. God
required of them a total trust and obedience and the acceptance at times of a dark and mysterious journey. This is
what we see when Abraham took his beloved son up the
side of the mountain to sacrifice him in obedience to an
apparent demand of God. We see this when Jesus Christ
walked around the base of that very same mountain to the
Praetorium, then to the house of the high priest and finally
to His death on Calvary. If you ever need any proof that the
intellect must be led on in darkness and conflict by the
mysteries of the living God, remember these two scenes of

[3]Rudolf Schnackenburg, *The Moral Teaching of the New Testament,*
3d ed. (London: Burns and Oates, 1982), 34. Also see Rudolf
Schnackenburg, *Belief in the New Testament* (New York: Paulist Press,
1974). This entire tract can be read with much profit.

sacrifice that took place in the same spot—Abraham and Jesus on Mount Moriah, which later became Mount Zion, with its little hill of Calvary.

Belief in Jesus as Healer

What kind of faith did Jesus demand? Several kinds. Initially He challenged people to believe in the powers of healing invested in Him by God. As Father Schnackenburg writes:

> He was able to use such belief as a starting point for Messianic faith, because healing, the driving out of evil spirits and other miracles forced the question of Messiasship to be raised. After he had taught in the synagogue at Capharnaum, and had exorcised an unclean spirit there, those present were thrown into great excitement: "What thing is this? What is this new doctrine? For with power he commandeth even the unclean spirits; and they obey him" (Mark 1:27). After the stilling of the storm, great fear fell upon them all, and they said to one another, "Who is this (thinkest thou) that both wind and sea obey him?" (Mark 4:40 par.). He skillfully repulsed the malicious accusation of his opponents that when he cast out devils he was himself possessed by Beelzebub, making it clear to everyone that here was "one yet stronger" who had "come from God" (Mark 3:22–27 par.). This is why Jesus accepted the simple faith in miracles, the "faith in the saviour", of the common people, when trust in God's envoy is awakened by it. The woman with an issue of blood had ideas that were still quite primitive regarding the power that flowed from Jesus, but she believed wholeheartedly that in Jesus the helping power of God had come to her, and Jesus assured her, "Daughter, thy faith hath made thee whole" (Mark 5:34 par.). The president of the

synagogue who called Jesus to his daughter's death-bed and then received the news of her death, was encouraged by Jesus with the words, "Fear not, only believe" (Mark 5:36 par.). In the case of the lame man it was the faith of his helpful friends which called forth from Jesus the absolution of his sins and physical healing (Mark 2:5). The question of faith is central to the narrative of the cured boy (Mark 9:14–29 par.): Jesus sighed over this disbelieving generation (v. 19) and reminded the boy's father that all things are possible to him who believes (v. 23), whereupon the man cried out, "I do believe, Lord; help my unbelief" (v. 23). Jesus let himself be moved by the great faith of the Syro-Phoenician woman to heal her daughter (Mark 7:29; cf. Matt. 15:28). He drew attention with especial praise to the faith of the pagan centurion of Capharnaum, who believed that by a mere word of command from afar Jesus could heal his sick servant (Matt. 8:10 = Luke 7:9).[4]

The conclusion cannot be denied that Jesus Christ expected faith in His miracles. Yet this faith is now denied by many educated people even in the Church. I think the denial of the miracles and signs of Jesus is insidiously undermining the faith of many Christians. Wonderful, scientifically unexplainable things happen today. It is simply a prejudice to deny without any thought of investigation that healing happens today. I know this because it happened in the life of Father Solanus Casey, whom I knew personally.[5] At Lourdes I had the opportunity to review sixty-four cases of medically

[4] Schnackenburg, *Moral Teaching,* 36–37.
[5] See T. Derum, *The Porter of St. Bonaventure* (Detroit, Mich.: Fidelity Press, 1968 [available through the Fr. Solanus Guild, 1760 Mt. Elliott Ave., Detroit, MI 40207]); also Michael Crosby, O.F.M.Cap., *Thank God Ahead of Time* (Chicago: Franciscan Herald Press, 1984).

unexplainable healings that had been accepted by the Lourdes Medical Bureau following very severe criteria of scientific inquiry.[6]

The Test of Faith

To deny the miracles of Jesus is not simply an intellectually shabby form of minimalism and an uncritical acceptance of contemporary scientific prejudice against what cannot be explained by present concepts of physical science.[7] It is something much more dangerous. It is to fail the first test of faith given by Jesus Christ in the Gospel. As Schnackenburg has pointed out very clearly, Jesus demanded that those around Him believe not only that He had performed works of healing but also that He could do so again and do so for them.

At times one hears the miracles of Jesus explained in purely symbolic ways: for example, that the curing of a man born blind was only a parable symbolizing Jesus' giving spiritual sight to the spiritually blind. It is well to recall that the person proposing that theory has failed to take into account the documented cases of scientifically inexplicable healing that occur in our time at Lourdes, where terminally ill patients have been rapidly and completely cured in a way that is totally inexplicable by scientific means. Faith tells us

[6] Medical reports and reprints from medical journals are available to all medical doctors from the Medical Bureau, La Grotte, Lourdes, H. Pyrenees, France (please send postage). Also, see Ruth Cranston, *The Miracle of Lourdes* (New York: McGraw-Hill, 1955).

[7] The educated reader is encouraged to read the illuminating article by Fr. Donald Senior, C.P., "The Miracles of Jesus", in *The New Jerome Biblical Commentary,* (ed. R. Brown, J. Fitzmyer and R. Murphy (Englewood Cliffs, N.J.: Prentice-Hall, 1990), 1369–73.

that they were cured by the power of God. Failing to recognize this fact is opening the door to the refusal to accept Jesus' physical miracles, which He proposed as the first step of faith. So important for faith is the acceptance of Jesus' power to heal that as recently as December 1987 the Holy Father reiterated the Church's belief in the Lord's signs and miracles.

The Pope was not hesitant to identify a "rationalistic prejudice" against the miraculous. This prejudice, which arises from basically simplistic understandings of physics and of the nature of matter as well as from secularism, is undermining the faith of millions of Christians in the more technologically advanced nations. While it is obvious that concepts such as divine power and the miraculous fall outside the parameters of science as it is presently defined, it is also true that scientific methods can be used to verify that something has occurred without any known physical explanation. While science properly used can neither affirm nor deny the act of faith, those who unscientifically attack religious belief on "scientific grounds" actually violate the laws of science that they pretend to follow.

The acceptance of well-documented historical facts is another matter. Simply to reject the account of Jesus' miracles because of prejudice or, even more absurdly, to explain them away by symbolic explanations is to undermine the first act of faith demanded by Christ:

> If we accept the Gospel account of Jesus' miracles—and there is no reason not to accept it other than prejudice against the supernatural—one cannot doubt a unique logic which links together all those "signs" and demonstrates their derivation from God's salvific economy. They serve to reveal his love for us, that merciful love which overcomes evil

with good as is shown by the very presence and action of Jesus Christ in the world. Inasmuch as they are inserted into this economy, the "wonders and signs" are an object of our faith in the plan of God's salvation and in the mystery of redemption effected by Christ. As facts, the miracles belong to evangelic history, and the accounts contained in the Gospels are as reliable as, and even more so than, those contained in other historical works. It is clear that the real obstacle to the acceptance of Christ's miracles as facts of history and of faith is the anti-supernatural prejudice already referred to. It is a prejudice of those who would limit God's power or restrict it to the natural order of things, as though God were to subject himself to his own laws. But this clashes with the most elementary philosophical and theological idea of God as infinite, subsisting and omnipotent Being who has no limits except in regard to non-existence and therefore the absurd.[8]

During the life of Jesus Christ there were certainly educated and cultured people who heard about His miracles from eyewitnesses. They did not believe. There were at times in the crowd educated people whom Jesus encountered. They saw the miracles. Apparently few of them followed Him. Paul, a man history must include among its geniuses, believed because of the gift of faith that he accepted. But some of the Pharisees and scribes saw the signs and refused to believe. Things really have not changed very much.[9]

---

[8] John Paul II, *Wonders and Signs, the Miracles of Jesus* (December 9, 1987) (Boston: St. Paul Edition, 1990).

[9] See Appendix Two, which gives an account of the case of Vittorio Micheli. The obvious principal reason why many reject the occur-

Faith in the One Who Was Sent

There is a second level of faith, which Jesus Christ demanded, and this is the faith most clearly required in the synoptic Gospels. This is the faith that calls for belief and trust in God and in Jesus Christ, His anointed One, Who brings us salvation. In bad times the prophets, especially Isaiah, had promised those around them who suffered that they would be saved at the end of the ages. Jesus offered this hope again, but in a totally new way, and He confirmed this offering by his acts and miracles. Christ wanted people to believe that He brought salvation promised by God. Starting with the cure in Capernaum of the paralytic whose sins were forgiven and going on to the challenge to the disciples of John the Baptist, Jesus challenged the Jewish people, who had been prepared by their Tradition to expect a Messiah as "one who was sent".

I have often been deeply distressed by the complaints of students, even seminarians, that they have been told that Jesus is not the Messiah. The following quotation from Schnackenburg sheds some light on this question.

> It has been questioned whether Jesus really required faith in himself. Leaving St. John's Gospel aside for the moment and speaking only of the synoptics, no such explicit demand can

---

rence of miracles in the New Testament is the false assumption that they do not occur today. Miracles are by definition rare, unpredictable and specifically religious events. For this reason science cannot directly deal with the miraculous. However, scientific methods may be used to identify a rare, unpredictable and ultimately inexplicable event in a religious setting.

be found in anything he said (as regards Matt. 18:6, see the better reading of the Greek at the parallel passage Mark 9:42). Yet in fact, it is everywhere present. Just as Jesus did not openly declare that he was the Messias (hence the so-called "Messianic secret"), so according to the synoptic Gospels he did not expressly require faith in himself as the Messias. But just as he wanted people to recognize him as the promised Messias by all he did (Matt. 11:3f. par.; Mark 8:27–30 par.), so too he wanted this Messianic faith to grow among the people and then find expression in a profession of belief in himself. It is clear from his discussion with his disciples at Caesarea Philippi that no other response of faith would satisfy him.[10]

Many times devout believers are distressed by what can be called minimalism. It is important to understand why practical spiritual problems may be associated with using the writings of biblical scholars. Between the literal naïve meaning of a biblical text and the informed analysis of a scholar there may be a considerable gap, although the scholar may be just as much a believer as the informed devotional reader. In fact, the scholar may have a far deeper belief since he has to work with faith through many challenges and with much exercise of prayer. Between this believing scholar and rationalists of many shades of unbelief there is a still greater gap. The effective biblical scholar is required on one hand to help the believer and on the other hand to engage in an intellectual exchange with rationalists and other ultraliberal writers. On one hand he may richly use the truths of faith and on the other he may have to work with "an irreducible historical minimum", to use the phrase of biblical scholar Father Raymond Brown, S.S. This leaves

[10] Schnackenburg, *Moral Teaching*, 35.

the believing scholar open to attack on both sides—an unenviable position that the devout believer should understand and respect. It is my impression that the careful scholar is often carelessly quoted by others.

The informed reader who wishes to use Scripture prayerfully and intelligently will find an excellent discussion in the *New Jerome Biblical Commentary* in the section on Christology written by Father Raymond Brown, S.S.[11] This dedicated scholar clearly takes the reader through the shoals and leaves no doubt that after a life of extraordinary study and research Christ is for him "true God of true God" as proclaimed by the Council of Nicaea.

It is most unfortunate that flippant teachers often communicate to students minimalist opinions verging on skepticism. They are known to present these as Church teaching or as fact. These teachers exhibit not only a lack of understanding of basic scientific principles of research but also a faith that is shallow at best. The fact is that if the natural sciences always proceeded on minimalist principles, there would have been no Pasteur, Lister or Einstein.

Admittedly many Jewish people had been accidentally misled in their expectations of the role of the Messiah. Many Christians are also misinformed today. It is important to note, as Schnackenburg does, that Jesus' challenge was not simply an emotional one, as some of the television evangelists would have you believe. Nor was it simply an intellectual one, as many contemporary Christian writers (who are often seen as overly intellectual) would suggest. Jesus Christ appealed to the whole person, to intellect,

---

[11] Raymond Brown, S.S., "Christology", in *The New Jerome Biblical Commentary,* ed. R. Brown, J. Fitzmyer and R. Murphy (Englewood Cliffs, N.J.: Prentice-Hall, 1990), 1354–59.

desire and will. "Let him who has ears to hear, hear it" (Mk 4:23). Any reading of the synoptic Gospels makes clear that Christ appeals to the whole person, to the mind, heart and needs of the people around Him.

And yet even this appeal is acknowledged by Jesus to be insufficient for faith in Him. He also makes two other essential ingredients of faith very clear in what He says. One is that faith must be revealed. "I praise you, Father in Heaven, that you have revealed these things to little ones and not to the wise and prudent" (Mt 11:25; Lk 10:21). Jesus states that God has revealed to Peter His true identity as the Messiah, that it has not been revealed by flesh and blood (Mt 16:17).

The second truth that Jesus proclaims is the moral responsibility to accept this gift of God so as to make it grow. For this reason He criticizes the apostles and others for having little faith, that is, for faintheartedness, fearfulness and a lack of enthusiastic response, especially in the face of difficulty. He challenged them to move mountains by their faith and to let it grow like a mustard seed (Mt 17:20–21).

How does one arrive at stronger or greater faith? By incessant prayer, which guarantees a favorable hearing (Mk 11:24). The parables of the unjust judge and the insistent neighbor are strong indicators that Jesus Christ expects His followers—you and me—to practice what we say we believe, even when we must persevere for a long time in prayer and suffering.

What more important message is there for an age needing reform than that both our minds and hearts accept God's gift of faith in Jesus Christ as our Savior? Many young people leave the Church precisely because they say they did not experience this summons in the Church in which they were baptized.

The Warning to Confess Faith

Finally—and this is a very important message of reform for our time Jesus threatened dire and everlasting consequences on those who did not live out their faith by proclaiming it for the salvation of the world. These absolutely terrifying words are found in one form or another in all the synoptic Gospels (Lk 9:26; and Mt 10:33). "For whoever is ashamed of me and my words in this adulterous and sinful generation, of him the Son of Man will also be ashamed when he comes in the glory of his Father with the holy angels" (Mk 8:38).

Faith in the Son of God

But finally we come to the pinnacle of the evangelical expressions of faith in the Gospel of Saint John. There are so many significant texts that one is forced to be selective or end up simply quoting entire chapters, for as this Gospel states, "These are written that you may believe that Jesus is the Christ, the Son of God, and that believing in him you may have life in his name" (Jn 20:31). There are many confessions, such as that of Martha, "I believe that you are the Christ, the Son of God, he who is coming into the world" (Jn 11:27). So many proclamations like the most celebrated one of all, "God so loved the world that he gave his only Son, that those who believe in him should not perish" (Jn 3:16). There are so many proclamations of divinity: "The Father loves the Son and has given all things into his hands" (Jn 3:35) and "Believe the works, that you may know and understand that the Father is in me and I in the Father" (Jn 10:38). And, finally, "That they all may be one, even as thou Father art in me and I in thee; that they also be

one in us, that the world may believe that thou has sent me"
(Jn 17:22).

These powerful quotations from Saint John indicate that in
this Gospel something else is expected beyond the faith described in the synoptic Gospels, although Dr. Schnackenburg
indicates his belief that this is an organic development.
Writing of Saint John's Gospel, he says,

> Here faith is the great single expression covering everything
> that Jesus requires of men. It is Christological faith, that is,
> the confession that Jesus is the Messias and the Son of
> God. . . . And even now this faith brings possession of eternal,
> divine life. "He who believes in me hath eternal life." For
> the early Church, the power of faith to save was the conse-
> quence of Jesus' claim to be the Messias. But Johannine faith
> is not merely recognition and assent. As Jesus' vivid encoun-
> ters with people whom he leads to faith show, [the faith he
> demands] is both trust and submission. The numerous
> professions of faith not only praise Jesus with many titles
> of majesty and dignity, but also reveal personal emotion.
> The decisive thing, however, remains acceptance of Jesus'
> claims. . . . The moral importance of faith lies in the fact that
> it has accepted the demand for repentance and requires
> obedience to the Son of God (3:36), by the following of his
> teachings. (8:31f., 51; 12:47f).[12]

It is worthwhile emphasizing at this moment of moral
relativism that Saint John's Gospel makes obedience to the
teachings of Jesus an absolute necessity for the believer.
Despite the fact that Jesus is always presented as ready to
forgive any of His followers or any other repentant person,
He nevertheless calls for loving devotion to Himself and
obedience to His moral teachings: "If you love me, keep my
commandments. . . . He who has my commandments and

---

[12] Schnackenburg, *Moral Teaching*, 41–42.

keeps them, he it is who loves me, and he who loves me will be loved by my Father, and I will love him and manifest myself to him" (Jn 14:15, 21).

Is there a Christian who seeks sincerely to follow Christ who has not been electrified by these words when their meaning first became clear? I recall as a teenager reading these words, and they became the foundation of my attempts at ongoing conversion. Although I was somewhat disconcerted when I later learned that some scholars taught that these words may not have been the very words of Christ as He spoke them, they are still the foundation of my battles with my sinful impulses and narcissism. It is the Christian Faith handed on by the Catholic Church that these words are inspired truth, that they represent, at the very least, the teaching of the very early apostolic Church in her efforts to summarize the teaching of the Messiah. Any teacher responsible for handing on the Catholic Faith who does not effectively communicate this message has failed dreadfully to fulfill his assigned role in the life of the people of God. Such teachers have unwittingly contributed to unbelief, and for this reason alone they should seek the road of repentance and personal reform. The responsibility of the teacher of the truths of faith at any level is an awesome one. It is especially so for the theologian. It is a task made sacred by the Incarnation itself, since the teacher of God's revelation brings together the eternal and the temporal, the divine and the human. The nature of this task and its profound incarnational roots are summed up beautifully by Joseph Cardinal Ratzinger:

> If we had space to follow these thoughts, we could show faith's fruitfulness, which does not violate the historical record but reveals its truth and is open to every genuine

truth. The unity of the person of Jesus, embracing man and
God, prefigures that synthesis of man and world to which
theology is meant to minister. It is my belief that the beauty
and necessity of the theologian's task could be made visible
at this point. He would be bringing to light the foundations
for a possible unity in a world marked by divisions. He must
seek to answer the question of how this unity can be recognized and brought about today. In this way he could be
contributing to prepare for that unity which is the locus of
both freedom and salvation. But he can only do this provided he himself enters that "laboratory" of unity and freedom of which we have spoken, i.e., where his own will is
refashioned, where he allows himself to be expropriated and
inserted into the divine will, where he advances toward that
God-likeness through which the kingdom of God can come.
Thus we have arrived back at our starting point: Christology
is born of prayer or not at all.[13]

The Refusal to Believe

Jesus repeatedly explained the puzzling disbelief of those
who rejected him by references to their moral guilt. They
perform works of darkness and shrink from the light (Jn
3:19ff.). If malicious unbelief often accompanied by hate
arises from the dark depths of the human soul, faith is a
grace and must be given by God. No one can come to Jesus
unless the Father draws him (Jn 6:44).

One of the astonishing things that Jesus says about faith,
which is very challenging to all, is that the way of faith lies
open to everyone. But many people refuse to follow it out
of human respect. These words should sink deeply into our

[13] Joseph Cardinal Ratzinger, *Behold the Pierced One* (San Francisco:
Ignatius Press, 1984), 46.

hearts and remind us of the moral obligation not only to say that we are Christians and followers of Christ but also to profess it strongly and fervently in the face of an unbelieving world.

> Nevertheless many even of the authorities believed in him but for fear of the Pharisees they did not confess it, lest they should be put out of the synagogue: for they loved the praise of men more than the praise of God. And Jesus cried out and said, "He who believes in me, believes not in me, but in him who sent me. And he who sees me sees him who sent me. I have come as light into the world, that whoever believes in me may not remain in darkness. If any one hears my sayings and does not keep them, I do not judge him; for I did not come to judge the world but to save the world. He who rejects me and does not receive my sayings has a judge; the word that I have spoken will be his judge on the last day. For I have not spoken on my own authority; the Father who sent me has himself given me a commandment what to say and what to speak. And I know that his commandment is eternal life. What I say, therefore, I say as the Father has bidden me" [Jn 12:44–48].

To Believe with All One's Heart

Our moral obligation is not simply to acknowledge intellectually that Jesus Christ is the Son of God. It is to embrace Him fervently as Savior with all our powers and emotions. May I request that you ask yourself these questions? Are we Christians in the contemporary world responding fervently and devotedly and fearlessly to the moral responsibilities of the Christian faith? Do we believe in the powerful acts of God that were done by Jesus Christ as healer of the human race? Do we accept Jesus as our salvation and Redeemer in the way we are so clearly called to do in the synoptic Gospels? Finally, do we strive to embrace Him with our entire being as the Light of the World and our only entrance into life with the Heavenly Father? Are we doing these things? Do we as the body of believers really embrace Christ? Or rather are we, in the contemporary Christian world, caught up in a comfortable adjustment that is lukewarm, pale, frightened and intimidated by the secularism of our time? I am asking very simply: Have we Christians sold out on faith?

The believer accepts the fact that divine Providence has given us the Sacred Scriptures as a special grace. They are not the words of men; they are the words of God. To treat them like the words of men, Cardinal Newman observes, is the height of rationalism:

> It is Rationalism to accept the Revelation and then to explain it away; to speak of it as the Word of God, and to treat it as the word of man; to refuse to let it speak for itself; to claim to be told the why and the how of God's dealings with us, as therein described, and to assign to Him a motive and scope of our own; to stumble at the partial knowledge which He may give us of them; to put aside what is obscure, as if it had not been said at all; to accept one half of what has been told us, and not the other half; to assume that the contents of Revelation are also its proof; to frame some gratuitous hypothesis about them, and then to garble, gloss, and color them, to trim, clip, pare away, and twist them, in order to bring them into conformity with the idea to which we have subjected them.
>
> Conduct such as this, on so momentous a matter, is, generally speaking, traceable to one obvious cause—the Rationalist makes himself his own centre, not his Maker, he

does not go to God, but he implies that God must come to him.[14]

We have to accept the words of Scripture as living words addressed to ourselves. While we use our intelligence and research to discover the best possible understanding and interpretation of these words as they were originally given, it is more important, as Schnackenburg points out, that intellectually and emotionally we embrace Jesus Christ as the Savior of the world. No study that is worthy of a Christian should ever interfere with that profound, human commitment to Jesus Christ, which He demanded of His apostles and hearers.

The Christian community in the Western world needs desperately to listen again to the opening of Saint Mark's Gospel: "Repent and hear the Good News." We need to listen to these words at the end of the Gospels in which Our Lord Jesus Christ powerfully challenges us: "Anyone who has my commandments and keeps them, he it is who loves me; and he who loves me will be loved by my Father, and I will love him and manifest myself to him" (Jn 14:21).

This manifestation of Christ is what we seek. If we make the goal of our lives to settle for less, then we cheat not only ourselves but also our brothers and sisters in the human family who wait for the salvation given by Jesus Christ. It is to cheat the Church now. It is to cheat the people of the future. The words of Christ are a fire cast upon the earth. They call us to consume ourselves in the public witness to Jesus Christ and in the living out of His commandments. Anything else is insanity; anything else is sin. The Christian world is now like a sleeping giant that has allowed itself to

[14] John Henry Newman, *Essays Critical and Historical* (London: Longmans, Green, 1895), I, 32.

be lulled to sleep by materialism, secularism and rationalism. Powerful spiritual voices of our time led by Pope John Paul II call us to awake to embrace Jesus Christ as the Savior of the world. What arc we going to do?

A Witness to Life

Recently I had the opportunity to meet a woman named Joan Andrews in the back of a church in Manhattan.[15] Joan has been in prison many times, subject to long confinement and humiliation as a protester against the proabortion laws in the United States. When I saw her in the distance praying quietly in the church, I knew who she was. Involuntarily, a feeling of reluctance came over me as I saw her sitting there with others in the church. This woman has suffered humiliation, degradation and imprisonment. She is a reproach to me, and I could feel myself being reproached. I said to myself, I almost hope that she is a sort of argumentative, contradictory kind of person so that I will be able to placate my conscience by saying that she gets some secondary psychological gain out of her protest. I happen to believe in the protest but tend at times to think that going to jail for long periods of time for the refusal to pay fines is overdoing it a bit.

The woman who faced me was very calm, quiet and gentle. She was neither argumentative nor aggressive. She was the last person in the world whom one would ever expect to see in prison or challenging civil authorities. I

[15] See Richard Cowden-Guido, ed., *You Reject Them, You Reject Me* (Manassas, Va.: Trinity Communications, 1988); and Joan Andrews with John Cavanaugh-O'Keefe, *I Will Never Forget You: The Rescue Movement in the Life of Joan Andrews* (San Francisco: Ignatius Press, 1989).

remembered my days in the civil rights struggle when I had met certain people like this who could protest in a very quiet, humble way. I was immediately impressed. As I sat in the back of the church talking to her I could hear the words echoing through my mind, "You will be dragged before governors and kings . . . and you will be hated by all for my name's sake" (Mt 10:18 and 22).

This woman is a deep believer in Jesus Christ. Her belief in Him is not abstract or something accepted in a mediocre way. It is an overpowering embrace. You may feel uncomfortable and so may I when we have to witness such faith, but we cannot escape Jesus Christ's challenge to be such witnesses to all who are willing to hear Him in the depths of their hearts. It may be true that you and I are not ready for such a witness, that we do not have the courage or the total dedication. But perhaps if we opened our hearts to Him Who is truly the Messiah, we might be able, even in this unbelieving time, to make some effective and clear witness to Christ. And that will be the beginning of our reform.

Chapter Five

THE CONVERSION OF THE EMOTIONS

The idea that emotions need conversion brings us to a most interesting and challenging part of individual reform and renewal. Most people have only a confused notion of what an emotion is. Therefore, before we consider the reform of our own emotional life, it is worthwhile to stop and consider what emotions are. An even more interesting question is the following: What do emotional terms, such as *love* and *anger,* mean when they are applied to God, who in no psychological sense of the word may be said to have emotions?

The Mysterious Emotions

Emotions are the link between the body and the mind, and if we are speaking in terms of the spiritual life, between the body and the soul. The reason for this is that our emotions have two essential components, one psychic and related to the psychological powers of perception, awareness, intelligence and needs such as those for affirmation and intimacy and one related to the body. This is because emotions are always accompanied by physical reactions in the body. Usually emotional reactions are related to small but powerful secretions of the endocrine glands, which cause changes such as a rise in blood pressure, heart-beat and so on.

Emotions are so complex that the exact nature of the linkage between body and mind is still one of the mysteries in psychology. For example, if you think of a number, such as four, you probably do not have an emotional reaction. But if you think of a negative event, such as the legalization of abortion, you have a reaction of anger or sorrow. If you think of the announcement that a friend has been honorably recognized, you probably experience a feeling of joy. These ideas have caused physical reactions. The total experience is called an emotion.

It is important to differentiate emotions from physical needs or appetites. Hunger, sexual desire and fatigue are not emotions. You may be happy to get a good meal when you are hungry, but then you have an emotion, joy, correlated to the fulfillment of an appetite for food. Part of the role of civilization has been to link respectable human emotions with the fulfilling of appetites so that people do not act like animals, driven simply by sensual urges. Nowhere is this more obvious than in the civilized and moral linking of sexual desire with tender emotions. We say that when people separate these two they are acting in an animalistic way.

The principal emotions are love, hate, fear, anger, joy and sorrow, and these have many subtle, distinct phases. For example, fear can range from terror to mild apprehension; anger, from rage to mild annoyance. Joy has many colors— from laughter to a gentle but profound sense of peace and security. Sorrow wears a hundred different shades of violet, gray and black.

Emotions must also be separated from desire. Usually we use the word *desire* to identify our awareness of complex human needs such as intimacy, recognition, success and self-awareness, separating these from biological appetites. This distinction is not always very clear or complete. For instance, the sexual appetite, which people share with all kinds of creatures, including birds, bees and, yes, even clams, is also deeply linked with needs such as intimacy and acceptance to make the very complex experience of human love. Usually we put together all these separate elements, some physical, some psychological and some even spiritual, into a single word—desire.

Now, to add another note to the confusing concept of emotion, what do we mean by spiritual emotions? The idea itself is confusing, since emotion, as we have seen, is rooted in glandular responses.

Suppose we say that we love God. This can be a conviction such as loyalty. We would rather die than betray God. We would risk our lives for the sake of the Gospel. But when we say we love God, we might also mean that when we pray or read the Bible we feel an emotion of fulfillment and joy. Or we could mean that we have a deep sympathy for the suffering of Christ on the Cross. Or we could mean that we are moved to generous giving to our neighbors in need because these suffering people represent Christ. One could mean some or all of these things at the same time. These emotions are based on biological reactions, but they are attendant upon religious experience.

But what does it mean when we say that God loves us? Does God weep or have joy? Certainly we cannot mean that the eternal Divine Spirit experiences a rise in His blood pressure or that His heartbeat increases. The Divine Being cannot be said to react in that way.

What I think we are saying with these anthropomorphisms (human qualities attributed to God) is that God's divine attributes are symbolically represented by people's emotional states. In the Judeo-Christian Tradition we are totally justified in doing this because our own Sacred Scriptures have used these analogies drawn from emotional experience and related them to God. Except for saying that God feels fear, our own sacred books apply all principal emotions to God's actions: love, hate, anger, joy, even sorrow. Yet we all know that insofar as people experience these things, they are only symbolically applied to God. They are not, however, symbolically applied to Our Lord Jesus Christ, Who was true God and true man. Christ did experience all of the emotions, even dread (which is part of fear), in the Garden of Olives.

An Emotional Binge

Having now thoroughly confused you, because if you are not confused about emotions you are probably wrong, we will look at the emotional situation in our own country and in the Church. It would seem appropriate either to say that in our age we are in a highly emotionally expressive situation, a high, or, if you are displeased with it all, that we are on an emotional binge.

In the past the United States, borrowing the manners of its parent country, England, was a somewhat emotionally repressed civilization. This can be seen in its choice of leaders and heroes. No one ever thought of Washington or Lincoln, or Wilson or Roosevelt, as particularly emotionally expressive. Most respected world leaders of our century in government and in religious organizations, business and finance and even the arts were thought to be rather level-headed and sparing in their emotional expression.

There are many exceptions, but even these exceptions felt compelled to operate within the bounds of reasonably predictable behavior, like the fire-breathing evangelists, the rough-and-ready cowboys and popular comedians. There was always room in America for Billy Sunday, Bishop Sheen and even Harry Truman, who could all express their emotions about things strongly but within limits.

Generally, Americans and most northern Europeans were expected to be a bit emotionally repressed. Since repressed behavior is now considered out of line, it is worthwhile to examine what repression is. True repression occurs when our emotional feelings and ideas do not even rise to the level of awareness. We are simply unaware of our emotions, although they may profoundly affect our conscious behavior. There is also partial repression when people hold back their feelings and emotions almost automatically but are aware that these feelings are operative, for instance, when they "swallow" an angry word.

Finally, there is something that is mistakenly called repression but is in fact conscious control. This is when people deliberately do not express what they feel. Perhaps they suppress it because good manners tell them to do this; for instance, when a preacher talks for too long, they repress a desire to shout out and tell him to sit down. People also repress things because of manners, which vary from country to country. Even within a culture the social expectations of people vary at times and places.

The important fact is that when repression, either partial or complete, is used too frequently or even brutally, psychological difficulties may occur. Repression is never completely successful over a long period of time. The pressure, as it were, builds up inside the psyche of the individual and is likely to burst out like steam out of an old boiler. It is much better if a person learns to resolve or deal with emotions consciously rather than to repress them.

We now have an interesting and spiritually significant phenomenon going on in American culture. The media and the pop psychologists are all giving the message that repression is bad. This is foolish, because repression and conscious control exist to temper and even at times to suppress reactions that may be inappropriate for oneself or dangerous to others. A society or an individual that is not capable of repression or conscious control is like a car without brakes. Too much repression is like driving with the brakes on.

The entertainment media in the United States and western Europe have assumed the task of forming the emotional life of children and teenagers. The media have become dangerously emotionally expressive, especially with extremes of horror, rage and despair and also of sexual desire. It would appear that the normal range of emotions has been exhausted, and entertainers anxious to sell their wares have moved beyond the civilized expression of emotion.

Think of Jimmy Stewart and Greer Garson and a host of other civilized entertainers, and then compare them to the present crop of rock stars, who blend horror, rage and sexual hunger into paroxysms of emotion that would have seemed totally ridiculous and repulsive only thirty years ago. We have moved from the rather harmless emotion evoked by the Beatles to the chaotic expression of what is called Heavy Metal. These degenerate forms of entertainment are so unrepressed sexually that people seem to require narcotics either to perform them or to "enjoy" them.

One must not confuse certain cultural changes with decline. The removal of excessive repression in American life has not been all bad. It has led to an informality and expressiveness in manner that can be more honest and more interesting. If nothing else, our contemporary political figures are slightly more exciting than Calvin Coolidge was.

Unfortunately, however, informality and emotional expression are so widespread now that we cannot enjoy an exception to the rule of repressed feelings such as Mayor LaGuardia provided in political life or Cardinal Cushing did in the religious sphere.

It may well be that the contemporary openness to feelings and emotions contributes to the widespread interest in spirituality. Even our topic, repentance, has strong emotional overtones. Such powerful religious movements as Marriage Encounter, Cursillo and the Charismatic Movement have been able to take root across the Catholic community only because of the removal of emotionally repressive structures. This is all for the best.

The removal of emotional inhibitions has also deeply affected the life of the Church. Recently, in Saint Peter's Basilica I came across a startling statue of Pope Pius XII. It powerfully represented the controlled personality of that great prelate. We have only to compare the presentation of self of Pius XII with that of John Paul II. Both of these men represent great talent, concern and dedication to the Church. But in the same pastoral position, one was expected to present himself in a highly controlled, aristocratic way, and the other has to be able to use and express almost every available shade of emotion. So our emotional age has its good side as well as its problems.

The Reform of Emotions

This brief discussion brings to mind the complexity of emotions and their effects on the individual and on culture. The question, "What does the reform of emotion mean?" has greater significance. What about the relationship between emotions and the kingdom of God? When we think about these questions, several obvious things almost leap out at us.

First of all, it must be the goal of the Christian not to suppress or repress emotions but rather to bring them back into harmony with divine revelation and Christian morality. In a word, if we are to follow the teaching of Christ, we must free the Christian from unhealthy repression so that these powerful forces can serve the Gospel.

Occasionally, ideas have come into Christian spirituality from the Greek and Latin stoic philosophers. Some of the Greek and Roman writers really thought that emotions were all simply sources of disharmony and of driven need and that the good Christian was a person without emotion or at least without emotional expression. There are too many examples in the Gospels of Our Lord giving vent to His emotions to make these stoical theories very convincing. There are saints from Paul to Francis and from Mary Magdelen to Teresa of Avila who richly used their emotions and who are clear witnesses against repressive ascetics in Christianity.

However, emotions are not in themselves either reasonable or capable of reason. This is the task of the intellect. Emotions are not intelligent in themselves. They need to be guided and directed by intelligence. This brings us to the forgotten truth in the contemporary confusion.

A Forgotten Truth

There is nothing intrinsically good about uninhibited emotions. They do not in themselves lead to either truth or goodness. This is because one of the effects of original sin was to throw emotional life into chaos. A life directed primarily by emotion is going to end in disaster. The Greeks had a saying, "Those whom the gods would destroy they first make mad with love", and by love they meant *eros,* or passionate, emotional love.

There is a modern superstition, totally unscientific but frequently proposed by pop psychologists, that the unbridled and uncontrolled use of emotion is the best guide for human behavior of either individuals or society. Dr. Donald Campbell, in his presidential address to the American Psychological Association in 1975, denounced the profession of psychology in the United States for this error and blamed it for undermining the characters of 80 to 90 percent of American undergraduates.[1] The lie is given to the theory that unbridled emotion is the best guide to human behavior by looking at the most emotionally uncontrolled and expressive leader of the twentieth century. At one time or another we all have heard the recorded voice of this man, who spoke with the unbridled emotion of hate. His name was Adolph Hitler.

The Christian must be guided by truth and not by emotion. "If you live in my word, you will be my disciple. You will know the truth and the truth will make you free" (Jn 8:32). Truth speaks first to the intelligence or mind of man and then through it to the emotions.

If our emotions do not correspond to truth in themselves, why use them at all? A fact that leaps out at us from our discussion of emotion is that emotions give us power. Emotions are linked intimately to our physical powers. The psychological powers of the individual, intelligence and mental functioning, are dependent on neurological and

[1] As cited in Paul Vitz, *Psychology as Religion* (Grand Rapids, Mich.: Eerdmans, 1975), 49.

physiological dynamics. Hence emotions are the fuel of life. No one ever died for an abstract idea, but many people have died for a truth in the mind backed up by a fire of emotion in the heart. Sometimes people have died for pure emotion, or for error that had emotions wrongly supporting it, but no one has ever risked his life or done any great task well without the sustaining energy of emotion.

Well-directed emotions are essential for any effective human endeavor. They are absolutely essential for productive and intelligent living of the Christian life. For this reason the Lord praised the lawyer who summed up the law by saying, "You shall love the Lord your God with all your heart, and with all your soul, and with all your strength and with all your mind" (Lk 10:25–28).

The soul is the mysterious, deep, mystical element of man that does not change. The mind is the intelligence. And the strength refers to the body with all its dynamics and powers. But the heart stands symbolically for the expression of emotion.

Popular Errors about Emotions

We see many Christians in our society misusing emotions. The following errors confuse the emotional life of believers and have done a great disservice to our culture and to the life of the Church. You might ask yourself if you have picked up one or another of these errors.

1. *Emotion is the best and sole guide of human behavior.* This error seriously undermines morality and says, "Do it if you want to do it." This is the very essence of contemporary selfism.

2. *Emotions are essentially uncontrollable.* This is the error of

"I can't". Certainly emotions are powerful. They often cannot be intellectually controlled or directed, as one knows from a temper tantrum or perhaps a love affair. But emotions can be subject to both intelligence and will. This control may take time and effort, and it may not have perfect results. However, the battles to control emotion, especially the emotion of anger, are called for very directly by Our Lord Jesus Christ, in the Sermon on the Mount, and in the parables of forgiveness by the three powerful New Testament writers John, Paul and James.

These writings contain serious warnings against anger and despair. Along with the Lord Himself they require that human relationships of any kind, including the relationship of marriage and family, be governed by intelligence and morality and not by a pagan indulgence of the emotional drive and feelings.

3. *The person who follows his heart is a sort of hero and is better than the person who has followed his mind along with his heart or even his mind alone.* This belief is the least obvious but most dangerous error.

In fiction and drama, even in the selection of popular heroes, the person who follows his heart is likely to win the greatest applause. An interesting example is Edward, Duke of Windsor, who abdicated his throne and his responsibilities as King to follow his heart and marry a divorced woman. The then-Primate of the Anglican church, Archbishop Lang, insisted that the Crown Prince abdicate if he intended to marry against what was then the law of his church. Overnight Edward became a hero. It must be said that the Windsors did spend the rest of their lives with dignity and poise, but they hardly are the stuff of which heroes are made.

The ex-King's younger brother, who admitted that he

was totally unprepared for the role, turned out to be a modest and admirable leader of his people in a terrible war. King George was guided by duty, reason and courage in the face of bombs and rockets. Bravely he remained in danger in London during the blitz with the royal standard flying, indicating that he was present. Yet the world admired his brother who had been led by emotion.

Emotions: The Power Sources of Behavior

Properly used, emotions are the power sources of moral and religious leadership. Few of us are inspired by those who merely live on ideas. Even if they are righteous people, they do not easily win the admiration of others because they hide their emotions. While some apparently emotionless people are virtuous, no one admires the detectives of the 007 type who are really emotionless caricatures of men contrived by the author.

But ask yourself, have you fallen into the error of admiring those who are led by heart alone? Often they are lopsided and essentially self-seeking people who, even when they seem generous and compassionate, are unguided by reason and can be led to dangerous self-indulgence and manipulation.

A Christian's Emotional Ideal: The Imitation of Christ

The well-balanced person is guided by intellectual insights and on the basis of these makes serious decisions. Emotions provide the fuel to follow through on these decisions. The good Christian will endeavor to be an emotionally well-balanced person and at the same time will rely as much as possible on the help of revelation and on the teachings of the Church, the assistance of the sacraments and the gifts of the Holy Spirit. No one has less excuse for a life of pure emotional indulgence than does the Christian. No one.

Our Church is founded by Him Who is the Word of Divine Intelligence and at the same time the Image of the burning infinite love of God for His children. The ideal is that mind, heart and will should be totally subsumed by and transcended into a life that is characterized by the simple phrase of Saint Paul, "The love of Christ urges us on" (2 Cor 5:14). We have an army of teachers of proper Christian behavior, from Paul the Apostle to John Paul II. If we refuse to listen to this wisdom and put in its place the latest trends of a pop psychology that is scientifically shabby, then of all men we deserve to be called fools.

Is there a word to sum up the integration of mind and heart, of intelligence and emotion, called for by the Gospel? Of course there is, and this word is *discipleship* or the *imitation of Christ.* This is the biblical answer to our question.

With Christ we must be enlightened and lead a life of loving concern for others, more and more aimed at the fulfillment of the kingdom of God in our own lives. Because we are not perfect, and He was perfect, we must be prepared to struggle, to fail, to try again and to be wise as a serpent and simple as a dove. The imitation of Christ is a more powerful and ultimately psychologically more effective way of being His disciple than the simple acceptance and implementation of His counsels as a way of life. Imitation goes beyond obedience.

The ideal of the imitation of Christ as far as possible by inward dispositions, and to some extent by outward details, had its earliest realization in Saint Paul. For him life was for, in and with Christ. It was Christ Who lived in him (Gal 2:119). He wanted the life of Jesus to be "made manifest in our mortal flesh" (2 Cor 4:11). We are now weak with Him, but we shall live with Him by the power of God (2 Cor 13:4). Saint Paul even made up compound words in Greek to express this close unity, which directly implied imitation or "modeling behavior", in the contemporary jargon of psychology.

Does this mean that we must go about in an obvious attempt to mimic the external behavior of Jesus of Nazareth as we get some impression of it from the Gospels? Obviously this would be ridiculous for most of us. Can a grandmother go about acting like a young man who was an itinerant preacher two thousand years ago? While there are people like Saint Francis who actually imitated Christ in a very literal way, this cannot be expected of all. Therefore, what does the imitation of Christ mean?

Obviously one must study the biblical idea of the imitation or following of Christ. This is an idea that was very significant only a few decades ago in the Church, and in fact, after the Bible the second-most-popular religious book in Christian history is called *The Imitation of Christ.* Although this book, like all other books, must be seen in the perspective of its time, it does call people to a profound and personal dedication of their lives to Christ and to an attempt to follow His example. Dr. Schnackenburg considers the idea of the following or imitation of Christ and gives us this important insight:

> Following is to be understood here as more than a moral attitude, as an actual imitation. . . . By his sufferings, Christ has given us an example so that we too may follow in his footsteps. There is nothing strange about this development,

for even in the relationship of Jesus' disciples to their master the idea of imitation was not wholly excluded. At least in one respect Jesus set himself as an example for them, in service and utter devotedness. "And whosoever shall be first among you shall be the servant of all. For the Son of Man also is not come to be ministered unto; but to minister and to give his life as a redemption for many" (Mark 10:44f.par.). . . . With perfect clarity [this imitation is expressed] in St. John's gospel, which records the symbolic act of the washing of the feet. "For I have given you an example, that as I have done to you, so you do also" (John 13:15).[2]

Schnackenburg sees this teaching on the imitation of Christ in Paul, in John and in the Apostolic Fathers, especially Ignatius of Antioch. As the direct worship of Christ grew, so did the desire to imitate Him.[3]

If we are serious about the imitation of Christ in our own lives we must clearly have in mind what He did when He lived in this world. He did not simply go around consoling people and working miracles that improved the lot of individual suffering souls. He preached the kingdom of God, and He fought a battle to the death against the power of darkness, against the prince of this world (Jn 14:30). No one can imitate Christ in His divinity or of himself do acts that require divine power. We cannot heal the sick or walk on the sea. But we can imitate Christ by expending our time and energy, our intelligence and emotion, in the same battle that He fought.

The battle in its contemporary phase is the focus of Pope John Paul II's encyclical letter *Dominum et vivificantem* of

[2] Rudolf Schnackenburg, *The Moral Teaching of the New Testament*, 3rd ed. (London: Burns and Oates, 1982), 52–53.

[3] Schnackenburg, *Moral Teaching*, 161ff.

May 30, 1986.[4] While writing on the Holy Spirit, the Pope sharply focused our attention on the imitation of Christ at a most personal level, the conflict with sin. Beginning with Jesus' proclamation that He will convict the world concerning sin, the Pope links these words with our time and world situation by joining them to one of the pivotal statements of Vatican II found in the Pastoral Constitution on the Modern World, *Gaudium et spes.*

The Council asks all Christians to focus their attention on the human family along with all of the realities in which this family lives:

> The council gazes on the world, which is the theatre of man's history, and carries the mark of his energies, tragedies, triumphs; that world which the Christian sees is created and sustained by its Maker's love, fallen indeed into the bondage of sin, yet emancipated now by Christ, who was crucified, and rose again to break the stranglehold of personified evil, so that this world might be fashioned according to God's design and reach its fulfillment.[5]

The Holy Father writes, "This very rich text needs to be read in conjunction with the other passages in the Constitution that seek to show with all the realism of faith the situation of sin in the contemporary world and that also seek to explain its essence."[6] The Holy Father then turns his attention to the words of Our Lord that the Holy Spirit will convince the world of sin and states that this text must be given the widest possible meaning insofar as it relates to all the sin in the history of humanity. He points out that

[4] Pope John Paul II, *Dominum et vivificantem* (Boston: St. Paul Books and Media, 1986).

[5] *Gaudium et spes,* no. 2, in Flannery Austin, O.P., ed., *Documents of Vatican II* (New York: Pillar Books, 1975), 902f.

[6] *Dominum et vivificantem,* no. 29.

Our Lord explains that sin consists of the fact that they do not believe in Him.

The Holy Father then teaches that this text assumes universal dimensions by reason of the universality of the redemption accomplished through the Cross. The mystery of redemption opens the way to an understanding in which every sin, wherever and whenever committed, has a reference to the Cross of Christ and therefore indirectly to the sins of those who willfully have not believed in Him and have condemned Jesus Christ to death on the Cross.

The Great Sin

The great sin of the modern world is the same as the great sin of the time of Christ. It is that in some way or other we all refuse to believe in Him. Not only the secular world but also we ourselves as Christians are constantly tempted to believe in Him less than we should, to put that belief into a secondary place in our lives and thus weaken our identity as devoted apostles. Faith in the biblical sense is not simply intellectual assent but an emotional, even passionate embracing of the truths of faith.

You and I are called at this moment in Church history to work against the forces of personified evil and individual human evil in the world. In some cases these forces operate through disbelief. But they also operate by intruding themselves through the imbalance of emotion and intelligence.

The influence of evil forces can be seen in our failure to use intelligence and will to make an act of mature faith. Evil also gains control by our failure to direct our emotions toward living and acting within the law of God.

This is a time for reform of mind and heart, of thought and emotion. It is a time for each one of us to ask if we live our lives guided by faith. Do we submit our intellect to the mysteries of God and live our lives emotionally in communion with God, or do we allow our emotions, which are already confused by original and actual sin, to govern our lives? The purely intellectual person and the purely emotional person, however virtuous, fall short in the way of authentic imitation of Christ. Even a sincere believer in whom emotion and intelligence are fairly well integrated may not lead a life inspired by the Gospel because complete dependence on the operation of grace and the gifts of the Holy Spirit is absolutely necessary.

Before we proceed to these other issues related to reform, you might ask yourself whether you are leading the Christian life as best you can. As an intelligent, well-balanced, integrated Christian, are you striving with mind and heart to give yourself completely to that inner reform that is called for when our Lord says, "Repent and believe the Good News"?

A Warm and Alive Christian

It might be helpful to give an example of the imitation of Christ. Back in the early 1970s, one of the warmest and most emotionally sensitive men I ever knew spoke to me of the need for the reform of the Church. He was in one sense an unlikely reformer, gentle and kind with a self-effacing sense of humor. He tried always to make people think well of themselves. His life seemed to follow an easy path to success, but his early rise to positions of responsibility was very much the result of an unbelievable capacity for work and a selflessness in the performance of duty.

Terence Cooke was anything but a repressed man. He enjoyed life and was deeply engaged in whatever was going on, be it Mass for the schoolchildren, a long meeting with the priests' senate, Benediction for the cloistered nuns or hamburgers for his friends on a picnic. Those who knew him well know that he could get annoyed, although one had to know him very well to detect the signs. (He waved a pencil at you when he was annoyed but did not raise his voice.) He was always a perfect gentleman, in Newman's classic definition, always seeking not to offend.

Yet he had an iron will and was not particularly disturbed when he had to go against the tide or even against the voices of his friends. The secret of this very well balanced person who lived a stress-filled life in turbulent times with enormous responsibility is simply the imitation of Christ. We all have different images of Christ drawn from different scenes in the Gospel and from the actual needs in our own lives.

Terence Cooke as a young seminarian and as a cardinal of the Church only sought to follow Christ as he thought of Him and prayed to Him. His Christ was a gentle, kind Savior calling all to the love of God. But Cardinal Cooke knew what everyone else knows who has tried to imitate the gentle Savior, that inevitably this following leads to the Cross, the best and most powerful school for learning the imitation of Christ. In the years of his terminal illness Cardinal Cooke fought to control his emotions, often put to the test by severe sickness and pain. The following incident was first told to me by the Jewish cameramen in a television studio. The Cardinal had taught them much about the imitation of Christ by a continued and even conscious contradiction of our emotional impulses and needs.[7]

[7] See B. Groeschel and T. Weber, *Thy Will Be Done* (New York: Alba House, 1990).

Some time after the secret onset of his terminal illness, Cardinal Cooke was to appear on television with a few mentally retarded adults in a charity appeal. He was so ill from a treatment that it was not certain until an hour before he was to appear that he could go at all. After the appearance the Cardinal greeted the studio staff as old friends, as he always did. Then he got on an elevator along with two sisters and the mentally retarded people. The elevator got stuck between floors. During the two hours that it took to get it down far enough so that they could crawl out, the Cardinal kept the sisters and their charges from getting upset by singing songs, telling stories and saying the Rosary. He was the last one out of the elevator, with cameras and reporters all around. He appeared to be in great spirits and profusely thanked the engineers who had released them. He was, unknown to all but his secretary, desperately ill at that time. It is my impression that such emotional control in the name of charity should be called heroic virtue. It is clearly the imitation of Christ.

Chapter Six

THE CONVERSION OF THE BODY

There is no doubt that the dignity and respect that once surrounded sexuality, marriage and the role of women and young people of both sexes in the United States and much of the world have all but disappeared. In the media every conceivable vice, crime, sin and form of lust is seductively and even violently presented. This is frequently done in a way that suggests what is called in moral theology *Scandalum Diabolicum,* or bad example given for the pleasure of seeing others fall into sin.

The results are catastrophic. One-half of all marriages end in divorce. Endless numbers of single parents face the responsibility of raising their children without the support and sharing of that helpmate in the natural arrangement of Providence given for that task. A majority of young people are deeply morally confused, and many are completely indifferent to moral values. Consequently, a growing number of people struggle with many forms of sexual conflict. And more and more of the children who manage to survive the public approval of abortion end up facing lives of loneliness and animalistic competition for a bit of pleasure that sexual indulgence affords. But this is not all!

The worst is that those who are supposed to preach the truth of Christian morality as founded on the Gospels and handed down by the Church through the centuries either are silent in the face of this anticulture or are actively participating in it. We Christians often fail to recognize what Pope John Paul II in his encyclical on the Holy Spirit called "anti-word" or "anti-truth".[1] This corruption of truth falsifies our relationship with God and leads us to place ourselves above and beyond His plan of salvation. This leads to what Saint Paul calls "making a god out of sensual appetites".

Sexual Confusion in the Churches

Not only does our society need a reform to turn it away from the deepening error that *sex is for fun,* but also the Christian churches need a reform because of their placid acceptance of this antimorality. Many Christian theologians— Catholic and Protestant—and among Protestants even a number of Evangelicals, have chosen to say little or remain silent in the face of an overwhelmingly hedonistic culture.

Some theologians and teachers of various Christian denominations, including a number of Catholics, have chosen the easy way out and have often endeavored to justify sexual misbehavior on the grounds of compassion, a quality that is necessary at any age, regardless of how good or bad its moral climate might be. Despite the explicit teaching of the highest pastoral authority of the Church, some theologians persist in teachings that can only lead people astray.

You are, of course, aware of many scandals. They make the headlines frequently, when priests, ministers, religious

[1] Pope John Paul II, *Dominum et vivificantem* (Boston: St. Paul Books and Media, 1986) no. 37.

or significant laity of various churches are known to have been involved in immoral behavior. Personally I consider this only the symptom of the disease. A much more frightening sign is the acceptance by theologians and leaders within these churches of a degenerate sexual morality. This is an indication that a radical reform is needed. An example of this was the highly controversial book *Human Sexuality,* commissioned by the Catholic Theological Society of America, which received the disapproval of the Holy See and had its imprimatur withdrawn.[2] Even though the withdrawal of approval took place several years ago, the ideas contained in this book continue to be taught in some Catholic seminaries and communicated to some Catholic congregations.

Like most people, for a long time I remained rather silent even though I disagreed. As a psychologist I was aware that some of our problems covering morality came from rather severe religious education in the past, a sort of angelism. I am also one among many religious people (not just Catholics) who suffer some effects of sexual repression, a simplistic attitude pushing sexual needs into the subconscious mind rather than facing them in the light of the demands of the Gospel and Christian morality.

When I wrote my book *The Courage to Be Chaste*[3] I tried to bring these issues of sexual morality into focus in a calm and practical way. This book was favorably received in Catholic and Protestant publications and also in one Jewish journal. Despite the sexual revolution, I have not changed my mind that traditional Christian teaching on sexuality,

[2] A. Kosnik et al., *Human Sexuality* (New York: Paulist Press, 1977).

[3] Fr. Benedict J. Groeschel, *The Courage to Be Chaste* (New York: Paulist Press, 1985).

although demanding and requiring prayer, humility and an active spiritual life, is a sensible and creative road to a well-integrated life.

However, I regret that in my book I did not shout out like the little boy in the story, "The emperor has no clothes." I should have shouted out, "America has no morals." The perfectly obvious fact is that Christians, including the clergy and religious, including myself, are not directly and uncompromisingly confronting the antihuman, personally destructive and ultimately wicked abuse of sexuality in the United States of America and in many Western countries. I am sorry to say that in many ways, Christians—clergy, religious and laity—are gradually becoming so jaded by the anticulture in which we are living that we are like a prayer group assembled on the deck of the *Titanic* sometime after the waters started to rush into the hold.

The Morality of the Gospel

Without in any way minimizing the impressive Tradition of Christian moral teaching elaborated by the Fathers and Doctors of the Church, a Tradition that has essentially been able to maintain its integrity while confronting an incredible number of challenges, I would for the moment like to consider the basic moral teaching of Jesus Christ Himself, as given in the Gospels. This teaching is, after all, the foundation of all that has been developed in the last two thousand years. In every time of moral crisis, theologians such as Augustine, Thomas, Alphonsus and countless others have returned to the evangelical foundation of morality. We should consider Christ's moral teaching in general and then look at His teaching on sexual morality.

On the one hand it is clear that Our Lord intended to lift the yoke of complex observances of the Law off the shoulders of the people. He said clearly that His yoke was easy and His burden light, a reference to the yoke of the Mosaic Law, a familiar Jewish expression (Mt 11:30).

Did this mean that Jesus taught that there were no moral norms, no laws in that sense? The answer to that question is given by Schnackenburg: "It was not Jesus' intention to turn men loose in lawlessness and license. On the contrary, he demanded more of them, absolute and unlimited obedience to the holy will of God: 'Seek first the Kingdom of God and his justice' (Mt 3:33)".[4] This central teaching of Jesus is the norm of behavior for all those who seek to enter the kingdom of God. Everything that stands in the way of this kingdom is a stumbling block and must be rooted out. "And if your right hand causes you to sin, cut it off and throw it away; it is better that you lose one of your members, than that your whole body go into hell" (Mt 5:30). "This saying alone is sufficient to show how radical moral obligation has become in the teaching of Jesus."[5] In this particular passage Matthew relates this saying specifically to sexual morality.

Perhaps the most stringent and demanding of all Jesus' precepts had nothing to do with sexual morality. It is his teaching about forgiving one's enemies and not taking revenge (Mt 5:38–48). This radical obligation of forgiving one's enemies and not taking revenge goes beyond all other moral systems then and now and certainly contradicts much popular psychological theory. According to Dr. Schnackenburg,

[4] Rudolf Schnackenburg, *The Moral Teaching of the New Testament*, 3rd ed. (London: Burns and Oates, 1982), 74.

[5] Schnackenburg, *Moral Teaching*, 75.

the purpose of all the teachings in the Sermon on the Mount that go beyond the Law is not to demean the Jewish Tradition. There were in fact rabbis who taught things similar to what Jesus taught even on forgiveness. But these teachings were more in the nature of counsels of spiritual direction or other possible moral opinions. Jesus clearly makes His teaching a coherent whole, and one will be judged by these obligations at the Last Judgment.

Schnackenburg states that "Jesus' concern was with a unified religious and moral message whose novelty resulted from the significance of the moment reached in the history of salvation".[6] The liberal biblical scholar Rudolph Bultmann is required to admit of the Sermon on the Mount, "In all these sentences one decisive demand shines out. The good that is a question of doing must be done totally. Anyone who does it a little laxly, with reservation, just so that a pinch of the outward precept is fulfilled has not really done it at all."[7]

People often object that the morality of the Gospel is impractical because Our Lord uses hyperbole or exaggeration. His strong statement about plucking out one's eye or cutting off one's hand if it is a cause of scandal is used to argue that His serious moral teachings are an exaggeration. As Schnackenburg writes,

> One must not, however, make use of this popular style of teaching, a favourite throughout the Orient, in order to detract from the actual demands it contains. Jesus was demanding that even the occasion of sin should be radically removed, that brotherly love should not be preserved in any merely external manner, but should extend even to the very impulses

---

[6] Schnackenburg, *Moral Teaching,* 76.

[7] Rudolph Bultmann, *Jesus,* 79, as cited in Schnackenburg, *Moral Teaching*, 76.

of the heart and the most secret thoughts, and should lead to renunciation of a real right to retaliation (Matt. 5:38–42).[8]

Jesus' demands given in the Sermon on the Mount were intended to reveal something about the divine will. He revealed a moral element more important than the letter of the Law, external action and natural human feelings. This new element consists, according to Schnackenburg, in unselfish love, extending even to one's enemies, after the example of the merciful Father as Jesus reveals Him. God is infinite in kindness—but He also demands a degree of love surpassing ordinary measures and necessitating severe self-testing and self-conquest.

Many Christian theologians have been confused and puzzled by the severity of the demands of Our Lord Jesus Christ. He clearly goes beyond the Mosaic Law and beyond what in philosophy is called the natural law. Some Protestant theologians believe that He has gone so far as to make the observance of His moral teachings impossible so that we will realize our absolute necessity of dependence on Him for salvation. This view is unacceptable in Catholic theology because it seems to be saying that God is tricking men.

Another Protestant position, one that is more in keeping with the thinking of our times, is enunciated by Bultmann, who maintained that the radical teaching of Jesus Christ on morality is that men are required only to do what they intelligently understand they are called to do.[9] But this cannot be true because Our Lord does not appeal to intelligence but rather to His own authority. "In the law it was said ... but I say to you". He does not argue with the

[8] Schnackenburg, *Moral Teaching,* 77–78.
[9] Bultmann, *Jesus,* 68, as cited in Schnackenburg, *Moral Teaching,* 80.

people in the Sermon on the Mount or try to convince them. Jesus announces what He knows God's will to be. This in itself is very revolutionary. According to the eminent Lutheran scholar Joachim Jeremias, the very foundation of Jesus' moral teaching is that we are called to follow His teaching because the kingdom of God is at hand.[10] Those who have seen the love of God at work in His Messiah must be convinced of the truth of Christ's beatitudes and follow God alone and for love of Him will rid themselves of all selfishness because the promised hour of salvation has struck. According to Schnackenburg, "Jesus has returned to the primordial will of God, unrestrained by conditions and difficult circumstances of this world, regardless of human weakness and hardness of heart, and has set out commandments of God, wholly free from any of the compromises of daily life, and sets them forth in their integrity as what God demands."[11]

It would be ridiculous, as Schnackenburg points out, to try to defend completely the validity of Jesus' moral demands on the basis of a philosophical morality. A few years ago a distinguished prelate of the Anglican church had been the chairman of a committee attempting to formulate a moral consensus among the people of England, believers and unbelievers of every stamp. This consensus was to reflect what everybody thought about what should be done or avoided. It seems to me that such a consensus is categorically contrary to what the New Testament represents as the moral teachings of Jesus. He was not interested at all in what everybody agreed about. He was interested in what He knew to be the will of God, even if this demanded such

[10] Joachim Jeremias, *The Parables of Jesus* (New York: Charles Scribners, 1963), 115ff.

[11] Schnackenburg, *Moral Teaching,* 80.

things as forgiving one's enemies. Dr. Schnackenburg sums up the essence of Christ's moral teaching in this illuminating paragraph:

> So then we must let the words of Jesus stand in all their severity and ruggedness. Any mitigation, however well intended, is an attack on his moral mission. But how Jesus judges those who fall short of his demands is quite another matter. His behaviour towards the disciples gives us an object-lesson on this point. He took back even Simon Peter, who denied him three times and yet was the leader of the circle of the twelve, after Peter had bitterly repented his actions, and he confirmed him in his position as the chief of the disciples and the shepherd of the sheep (cf. Luke 22:32; John 21:15–17). Admonition and mercy are found together. It is the mercy of God which always comes first. It comes definitively into history with the person and works of Jesus. But Jesus also longs to awaken the ultimate powers for good in those laid hold of by the love of God and saved from eternal ruin. They should now thankfully do the holy will of God in its totality, unalloyed. If in spite of everything they again succumb to human weakness and wretchedness, God's mercy will not fail if they turn back in penitence.[12]

Christ's Teaching on Sexual Morality

Now how do we apply these rugged teachings to sexual morality? The answer is to be found in the Gospel itself. Before we come to the teaching of the Gospel, we must pause for a moment to consider sexual morality. The weakest link in the moral fiber of any person is usually sexuality. This is indicated in classical literature as well as in the Jewish

[12] Schnackenburg, *Moral Teaching,* 88–89.

Scriptures. It has also been made clear in serious writings from Saint Augustine to Sigmund Freud. People who criticize the Church for being preoccupied with sexual morality should recall this fact. Smart sayings such as "the Church should stay out of the bedroom" are offered by people who fail to recognize that a great many mishaps of human history have been rooted in the abuses of sexuality.

The sexual teachings of the Church are "rugged", to use Schnackenburg's word, but they are a logical extension of the teachings of Christ in the Gospel.[13] Is it more difficult to remain chaste than it is to forgive one's enemies or to strive to enter by the narrow gate? Most of us probably skim over many of the moral teachings of Christ, His commands and His counsels. The obvious ones that are difficult to ignore are the ones that pertain to sexuality, especially His very demanding requirement that one not consent to illicit sexual desire.

In one of His most powerful and uncompromising statements in the Sermon on the Mount, Jesus teaches the following: "You have heard that it was said, 'You shall not commit adultery'. But I say to you that anyone who looks at a woman lustfully has already committed adultery with her in his heart" (Mt 5:27–28). There follows immediately in Matthew, as we have previously noted, the hyperbole about plucking out one's eye or throwing away one's hands if these lead to sin. Christian Tradition has seen these statements as referring to a sexual desire that is knowingly and freely consented to and not as referring to the natural impulse of sexual need.

There are two practical observations to be made here. The first is that generations of sincere Christians, especially

---

[13] Schnackenburg, *Moral Teaching,* 88.

in the early decades of life, have struggled with this teaching either because they were not told what the distinction is between involuntary sexual impulse and lustful desire or because in the actual moment they were not sure what they were experiencing, impulses or consent.

The second point to be borne in mind is that the distinction is still not being made despite huge volumes of writing and psychological speculation on sexuality. The present confusion seems to arise from the muddled idea that all sexual desires are harmless impulses to be indulged, if possible, and that in the sense of the Gospel few if any of these are lust. We seem to have come from puritanism to libertinism without a stopover at common sense.

The fact is that the Gospel teaching is obviously a challenging one and by logical extension covers all illicit sexual activity and not simply adulterous desire. Saint Paul and the Fathers of the Church had no trouble developing a code of sexual morality from this one teaching. Admittedly they were also influenced by the Jewish Law and even by philosophical ethics, and by their observations on the sexual misdeeds of their contemporaries and the devastating results of moral misbehavior in the Roman Empire and after it. There can be little doubt that the austerity of Christ's teaching fitted in quite well with His whole emphasis on the totality of one's commitment to the kingdom of God.

Jesus and Women

The proscription against illicit desire in the Sermon on the Mount does not reveal Christ's motive for His strict teaching on sexual morality. Paradoxically, this motive is revealed by something entirely different, almost contradictory, and that is His attitude toward women who were "sinners". Many writers have already shown that Jesus' attitude toward women was one of high esteem and delicate tact rarely encountered in later Judaism.[14] He clearly took the religious aspirations of women seriously, and women responded to Him with loyalty and warmth. It is no accident that those who remained faithful to him to the end were, with a single exception, women (Lk 23:27ff.; Jn 20:25ff.).

But we learn the most about Jesus' attitude toward sexuality from His treatment of those women who were considered sinners by their contemporaries. Despite the fact that Jesus strongly defends marriage and family life (Mt 5:32; Mk 10:11) and declares marriage to be indissoluble (Mt 19:3–6), He shows an unexpected and at times, to some, scandalous regard for sinful women. The case of the woman who was a sinner "and whose sins were many" is a clear example (Lk 7:36–50). Jesus praises this woman "for she has loved much", and He forgives her sins.

An even more unusual incident is that of the Samaritan woman at Jacob's well. This woman, who had five husbands and was living with a man to whom she was not at the moment married, was given a profound spiritual teaching about the living waters of Jesus and the necessity of religion's having its origin in spirit and in truth (Jn 4:1–42). Despite the fact that many scholars believe that the author of the Gospel uses this incident to express some of Jesus' most profound teachings, there is no need to doubt that indeed He did have a kindly and respectful encounter with this poor woman who represented the traditional enemies of Jews.

Perhaps no incident reflects Jesus' basic respect for all, no

[14] Schnackenburg, *Moral Teaching,* 132ff.

matter how debased or unfortunate, more than the account of the woman accused of adultery (Jn 8:1–11). His startling words at the end of the incident should be taken very seriously: "Neither do I condemn you; go and do not sin again." We must ask why Jesus Christ, who calls us to repentance and holiness of life, offers praise to a sinful woman at a banquet, offers "living water" to a many-times-married woman living with another man and saves a woman condemned for adultery who did not seek Him out with repentance but encountered Him by apparent happenstance on the way to execution. The answer is that Jesus loves all the children of the Father and has come to seek and to save those who are lost (Lk 19:10).

If Jesus' loving concern extends to these sinners and, in fact, even to His executioners, for whom He asks forgiveness (Lk 23:34), then every follower of Jesus must show love and respect to all. The root of all lustful behavior is a lack of respect. Lust uses others' bodies (or even one's own body) for gratification without regard to the needs or rights of others or to the Law of God. Sometimes this disregard is complete, as in prostitution and pornography, but at other times the lack of respect is mixed with love and affection, as in premarital sexual relations.

It is obviously true enough that lust and love can be mixed in the same relationship. But this does not make it right. It is also true that those with driven sexual needs may not want to use another person as an object of lust, but that is what they do in spite of their own sincere remorse. Even basic self-respect is often devastated by a powerful desire for sexual release.

Love and lust, kindliness and exploitation, affection and self-indulgence are all mixed together in this fallen world. But the Good News of salvation is that the Son of God nevertheless loves and respects all His brothers and sisters and calls them to repentance and reform.

Jesus' Love and Respect for the Individual

A summary of Christian moral theology on sexuality goes beyond the scope of this book. We have only asked the question concerning the foundation of Christ's moral teaching. It is love and respect for the individual. Since the first days of the Church there have been troubles, serious troubles, with sexual morality (see 1 Cor 5:1-2). But these troubles have not caused the Church to back off from the basic teaching of Christ. In our time there is indeed a dreadful lack of respect for women, for children, for marriage and family, for sexuality, for everyone. No matter how much trouble a person may have trying to live up to Christ's teaching, a constant meditation on the respect that should be shown to all will be the beginning of a salutary reform.

The Girl Who Had Nobody

For some years, I have had the privilege of working with an extraordinary young man, Chris Bell, who has opened and directs several homes for homeless mothers and their babies. The staff and volunteers of the Good Counsel Homes represent an attempt to assist young, homeless mothers to get a good start in life. Sometimes this means breaking a chain of sexual exploitation of the poor that has gone on for generations.

One Thanksgiving all the girls and babies and the sisters and lay workers who work with them came out to our retreat house for dinner. A small, quiet girl named Candy asked if she could speak to me. We went into the chapel with her little baby, who was about six months old. She told me that the baby's name was Esther, a rather old-fashioned name.

In the course of our conversation I asked Candy how she had come to our home. Her story is one of utter lack of respect for a human being. She told me that when she was two her father had taken her away from her mother because she was a drug addict. At fifteen Candy became a throw-away child. As she said, "I got kicked out by my father and stepmother." Her answer to the question of where she went is deceptively innocent: "I lived here and there on the west side." This means prostitution. Eventually she met a fellow who wanted to marry her, but they had no money for an apartment. He was caught holding up a liquor store to get money and was sentenced to prison for several years. Candy reported, "He told me not to wait for him." The baby was on the way. Through Covenant House she obtained assistance while having the baby and then came to Good Counsel, where she could stay for two years—time to get job training and for the baby to be old enough to go into day care.

When I asked Candy if she had any family, she replied, "No". I responded that everyone had some family. Did she have grandparents, aunts, uncles, brothers and sisters? "No". I said, "You must have someone." With a childlike spontaneity she quickly held up her baby and said, "I have Esther." I have never quite recovered from this answer.

How easy it is for our society to dismiss this girl as a "streetwalker" and to pass judgment that her child should have been destroyed in her womb! How easy it is to reduce

Candy and Esther to a statistic! This is as cruel, but not as personally involved, as buying or selling her on the street. It is the rare society, even in Christian history, that has not done this to the poor and weak. It is the rare society that has not laughed at the girl in the street and called her victim child by unkindly names. It is a rare society indeed that has not piled up all its guilt on sexual addicts, people whose own background has cast them into the compulsive abuse of sexuality that has made them both the culprits and the victims at the same time.

The Key to Sexual Reform

As so often happens, it is the victims who can show the way out of these curses that society brings upon itself. In recent years a twelve-step program called Sexaholics Anonymous has grown out of the AA experience.[15] Along with several other movements that recognize sexual compulsion as an addiction, this group calls its members to "sexual sobriety", which generally follows the norms given in the Gospel. The basis of this sobriety is respect for self and for others. Could not this same respect be the foundation of a sexual reform in our contemporary society? Quite apart from any particular sexual sin, addiction or deviation, an intelligent approach to chastity is based on respect for self and for others. This respect is raised from an ethical stance to a supernatural virtue by reason of the fact that one accepts Jesus Christ as a teacher of justice and the Savior. Any poor sinner struggling and falling into any sexual problem can always find

[15] For information on Sexaholics Anonymous, write to Box 300, Simi Valley, CA 93062.

the way back through loving respect. It did not take Jesus Christ long to call sinners to repentance. He showed them a loving regard and told them to avoid sin. No better foundation can be found for a contemporary Christian call to sexual reform.

Chapter Seven

THE CONVERSION OF THE EGO

The words *ego, self* and *person* are used in many ways by different authors and at times by the same author. Sometimes these words mean a good to be enhanced or an evil to be overcome or just something indifferent. In America we have been involved for at least two decades in a remarkable age of self-centeredness or selfism. Professor Daniel Yankelovich in his book *New Rules* has critically identified selfism as the destructive ethic that puts oneself first in everything. The selfist is prepared to sacrifice the welfare of others for his own fulfillment.[1] Selfism also generates a magical idea that in some way the world owes it to me to fulfill all my desires and potentials. Selfism is obviously a philosophy of life that leads to isolation, loneliness and eventually a bitter rejection of life, which can never live up to the selfist's expectations. Selfism is deeply opposed to the spiritual principles of most world religions, and it is particularly opposed to biblical values.

As a personal attitude of life, selfism is often called narcissism, after the mythical Greek shepherd who fell in love with his own image in a pool. Thinking it was a god he saw, Narcissus drowned trying to embrace his own image.

[1] Daniel Yankelovich, *New Rules* (New York: Random House, 1981).

125

Our society has been called a culture of narcissism.[2] This intense preoccupation with self inevitably leads to a kind of isolation and denial of community responsibility. Selfism is growing stronger in our culture and has been identified by Robert Bellah and others as leading to a form of individualism that is a socially destructive force.[3]

In contrast to the "self", when I use the word *ego* in this chapter I will mean the self I think about when I am asked to reflect on the inner life, or even the self that perceptually organizes everything around me, insofar as it pertains to me. Selfism, narcissism and egocentrism are all the diseases that distract the ego from its task of organizing reality for survival and growth. The Christian faith and most other world religions teach that the individual survives death. In some sense this ego, or person, must be gradually purified of selfishness and narcissism in life and even after death, so as to come to what Jesus calls "My Father's house".

A good life touched by grace may well be understood as the purification of the ego of its many spiritual illnesses, among them selfism and narcissism. In Scripture the superficial complex of self-centered values that opposes the authority of God in favor of the sick ego is called the world. The values of the world are identified in the First Letter of John as sexual lust, worldly desire and pride (1 Jn 2:16). The true disciple is described by Christ as denying his very self and carrying his cross (Mt 16:24). Consequently, as we have already seen in the opening chapters, the process of ongoing repentance and reform is a denial of the self or the sick ego.

[2] Christopher Lasch, *The Culture of Narcissism* (New York: W. W. Norton Co., 1979).
[3] Robert Bellah et al., *Habits of the Heart* (San Francisco: Harper & Row, 1986).

This reform or conversion is best carried out in a positive way by generosity and love. A loving reform not only will be more palatable to the refugees from contemporary selfism but also will deliver us from most of the worst effects of spiritual self-centeredness. Unfortunately there are ways to do battle with the self that only make it stronger and a more insidious enemy. The ego sick with selfism is best treated by the conversion of charity and love.

Jesus, Teacher of Love

It has been said countless times in the last two millennia that Jesus Christ was the teacher of love. He called for love of God and love of neighbor, love of friends and enemies, love of those close to us and love of strangers. Paradoxically, He even called us to love ourselves. And this is all true.

It has also been said that the foundation of His moral teachings is love, that He saw all morality from the viewpoint of love. In recent decades theologians have grappled with this idea and are attempting to formulate a moral theology based on Christ's command of love. And it has not been easy, because love means many things. Love can be a rationalization. Things have been done out of love that are clearly contrary to all human concepts of love. People have killed and been killed out of what was called love.

How, then, can we take a vague principle such as love and make it the basis of morality and justice? This has been a problem ever since Our Lord taught that the whole Law was summed up in two commandments: "You shall love the Lord your God with all your heart, and with all your soul, and with all your mind, and with all your strength . . . and . . . your neighbor as yourself" (Mk 12:29–31).

We live in a time that has come to use the word *love* very loosely. People sentimentalize their self-indulgence and call it love. In friendship and marriage, even in religious community life, people constantly talk about love. To use Saint Augustine's laconic phrase, we moderns are all "in love with love". I once went to a gloomy deserted building. It had once been the thriving novitiate of a vibrant and well-educated religious community. I went into the chapel. The tabernacle door was open. The sanctuary lamp was long extinguished. On the wall hung a felt banner in faded baby blue. In pink letters it said "luv". On the other wall, hanging askew from a tack in a corner, was a pink banner with the word *joy* in baby blue. Whatever this brand of love was, it did not ultimately bring joy to the people who owned that chapel. Almost everyone in our time wants to be thought of as a loving person. Once men presented themselves, probably with a good deal of vanity, as being tough. Now they want to be thought of as loving. Women also presented themselves as being devoted and faithful despite all obstacles. But now they prefer to be thought of as loving, even when love may not mean fidelity. Our enemies are always thought of now as being unloving. Anyone who is stern, even though just, is thought of as mean and unloving. What is more frightening is that people think it is loving not to tell the truth. People lie to cover up the truth and say that they did it out of love.

Agape and Eros

Because of all this confusion about the meaning of love, I would like to invoke the ancient distinction between love and charity to differentiate the two. Charity, which in

Greek is agape, is often translated by the word *love*. Charity means a love that needs to cherish, to put a great value on what is loved, to sacrifice for it. In this sense a man may be said to love God or to love his family. In the true sense of agape, or charity, we cannot be said to make our motive the fulfillment of our own desires but rather the good of that which we cherish. So if we say that we love music or money, that is not charity or agape but something different. It is a kind of eros. This is a love that fulfills our desire. Eros is not always evil by any means. It flows from human need. There can even be an eros for holy things such as a love of sacred music or the contemplation of God. Saint Augustine spoke of this when he said of God, "I have tasted you and I thirst for more." But when eros gets out of control, when it dominates, then it becomes hopelessly self-centered and consequently very dangerous.

The Greeks had a very strange play called the *Bacchae* about some women of Thebes who worshipped at the shrine of the Night. Night was a goddess who sent her son, Eros, to be their priest. He got them into a terrible frenzy of desire and lust so that they ended up killing and cannibalizing the men of their town, whom they said they loved. This is a revolting story, but if you go into your friendly neighborhood record store, you will discover that there are all sorts of albums that make the women of Thebes look very sweet and gentle indeed. When we surrender to eros in an unbridled way, we open the door to cruelty and the destruction of the very object we say we love.

Eros is at its best and worst the fulfillment of desire or of any need. It can be a need for what is passing or for what is eternal.

The love about which Jesus is speaking does not cancel out human need, nor does it condemn eros in all its forms.

Jesus Christ would certainly condemn eros when it seeks something excessively or at the expense of another, whether that other be God or a person. But when Jesus speaks of love, He almost always means agape, the love that seeks the good of the other, the love of generosity and of giving. In Jesus' teaching the giving of oneself is the essence of the love called agape or charity.

Our Lord, like the teachers of Israel, said that the love of giving is to be found first of all in God Himself. Jesus saw agape in His heavenly Father. "God so loved the world that He *gave* His only son" (Jn 3:16). Jesus often goes on to demand of His disciples that they give without hope of personal reward or repayment: "If you love those who love you, what reward should you have? Do not even tax collectors do the same?" (Mt 5:46).

Because Jesus is Messiah, He must consistently be seen in the context of the One Who has come to save a lost world. "And if I be lifted up from the earth, I will draw all things to myself" (Jn 12:32). In a lost and fallen world love will always mean self-sacrifice. "Greater love than this, no one has but to lay down his life for his friends" (Jn 15:13). No one should expect to be a true disciple of Jesus Christ and not constantly encounter demands for self-sacrifice and self-giving. "If anyone will come after me, he must take up his cross every day and follow me" (Mk 8:34). Charity must be accompanied sooner or later by pain and loss, by self-sacrifice.

Love of God as Taught by Jesus Christ

The phrase "the love of God" raises several questions: What does Jesus mean by the love of God? In His sense, how well do we love Him? And what does He mean by love for our neighbor, and how will we love our neighbor? I do not ask these questions in a vacuum. I must ask them in the very complex religious and social situation in which I live right now. My answers reflect some of the deeply moving scholarship on this subject by Rudolf Schnackenburg (see Chapters Two and Four).

There is unquestionably an enjoyment or spiritually erotic aspect to religious practice. Because there is a beautiful and ennobling aspect to the love and worship of God, religion has evoked some of the greatest works of human creativity. If you were able to take time to enjoy all the religious art and music in the world, you would be busy for a long time. Even apart from these works, there echoes in the souls of most men the sentiment of the Psalm, "I have loved, O Lord, the beauty of your house and the place where your glory dwells" (Ps 26:8).

In our culture religion has definitely become something to be enjoyed, not to be done out of duty. "I don't go to church because I don't get anything out of it. Why should I pray? God knows I try to be good and that I love Him." These often heard comments reflect the kind of thinking that is absolutely out of harmony with the teachings of Jesus about love of God. Jesus teaches that we must love God above all things for Himself, with agape, even though a fulfillment of our need for Him is part of our love.

Agape is also essential, while the fulfillment of the need for spiritual experience may not be. (Two passages in the Sermon on the Mount are devoted to the necessity of prayer: Mt 6:5f.; 7:21f.) Jesus Himself observes the law of the Sabbath, and when He criticizes the Pharisees on the point of activity on the Sabbath it is only to emphasize that their observance is so strict as to be inconsistent with other spiritual responsibilities (Jn 5). He also teaches that mere external religious acts are not sufficient. We must worship God in spirit and in truth (Jn 4:24). Worship is a loving duty to God, not primarily an aesthetic experience.

While Jesus Christ recognizes and reinforces the human impulse to ask God for what one needs, the focus of His prayer is God's kingdom, that it will come and that His will will be done on earth as in heaven. Jesus' intercession is focused on the same good as His preaching and His whole life—the reign of God over the hearts of men.

Even when Jesus speaks about prayer of intercession for our daily needs He demands a form of agape called trust. Jesus' own love for the Father always includes a loving confidence in Him. He only once directly speaks of loving God, when He preaches the two great commandments. But He often calls His hearers to confident trust or faith in God. We seldom think of it, but the greatest act of worship for the Christian is to trust God.

The religion of Jesus is one not only of trust but also of obedience, a form of agape. His life and death are a single total act of obedience to God. "I do as the Father has commanded me, so that the world may know that I love the Father" (Jn 14:31).

It must be said that Our Lord was totally loyal to His own Jewish heritage when He placed so much importance on acts of religious worship. Some people disparage religious worship and fail to pray publicly and privately because they think they are practicing a religion of Christian love that they have concocted for themselves. But they are simply out of harmony with the Messiah they say they follow. Jesus of Nazareth not only observed the Sabbath but also observed all the laws of the very religion He was to transcend as its Messiah. Where does Jesus preach most often? In the Temple. And what does He do when He is at rest, at work, in sorrow and on the verge of death? He prays to His Father. This is agape expressed as the fulfillment of religious duty.

As a child, Jesus had no doubt heard of the great Jewish martyr Rabbi Akiba. When this saintly rabbi was being taken out to his terrible death—to be flayed alive with iron combs—he realized it was the time to recite the ancient prayer the Shema. He recited it as he was being tortured to death, and his disciples shouted, "Enough!" He answered, "My whole life I have been concerned to say this prayer with my whole life and soul. He is taking me away from life; I will say the prayer while I still have life."[4]

Christians of our own time must stop and ask if they pray with fervor, devotion, constancy and regularity. One of the lost virtues of our time is reverence. A person who relates to God with reverence ennobles himself, even if he is struggling with a great fault. It is said of the Messiah that He prayed with a "loud cry and tears" and that He was heard because of His reverence (Heb 5:7). Can the Christian seeking to reform his life do any less than try to show the reverent and prayerful agape or love of God that the Savior so reverently practiced?

The Love of Neighbor as Taught by Jesus Christ

Our Lord linked the love of God to the love of neighbor. According to Schnackenburg, our neighbor includes the person closest at hand, the person with whom we are

---

[4] See Rudolf Schnackenburg, *The Moral Teaching of the New Testament* (London: Burns and Oates, 1962), 94.

involved here and now,[5] whether or not it is convenient to us to be concerned with this person. This is best illustrated by the parable of the Good Samaritan. This is something for us to be conscious of. We live in a time when every decent citizen is socially expected to give something to a cause or agency that serves the needy. This can be done conveniently and even with a tax deduction. Such almsgiving is good, but the parable of the Good Samaritan requires us to respond to the needs of the person right here in front of us, even at the risk of personal inconvenience and without expectation of gratitude.

It is not too much to say that according to Christ the love of neighbor can be equated with or take the place of direct service of God. But Jesus makes even more demands in the name of charity. We are expected to deal with others as God has dealt with us. This is the meaning of the parable of the unforgiving servant (Mt 18:23–35). Schnackenburg comments pointedly on this parable, which we so easily forget:

> It is on the foundation of this utterly resolute love for God that love of the neighbour is built up. Hence unbounded and genuine, heart-felt forgiveness of our brethren is a primary duty. The parable of the merciless servant (Matt. 18:23–35) demonstrates that God's infinite mercy is given us in the expectation that we deal mercifully with our fellowmen.
>
> The metaphor of the remittance of debts, applied here to forgiveness of spiritual guilt, is also used in the Lord's Prayer.... Thus behind the king, God is to be seen, and behind the punishment, eternal damnation. This parable itself shows that our love for our human brethren is in fact

[5] Schnackenburg, *Moral Teaching,* 102.

only an answer to the love of God, a passing on of his mercy.[6]

Jesus not only requires forgiveness; He also requires compassion or physical works of mercy. We are all deeply impressed by the verses of Matthew 25, "So long as you did it to the least of my brethren, you did it to me." The duty of helpful charity, of agape, is absolutely binding on us who believe in Jesus. Christians have no way out. We must do these things willingly and cheerfully. We must do them to the person at hand, the person whose needs are presented to us. If we fail to do them, we face condemnation at the Last Judgment. Schnackenburg points out that Christians are not simply called to be generous, to give a certain percentage until we feel comfortable that we have satisfied all our obligations. We Christians have an obligation to give in two ways often overlooked.

1. We Christians must give even when it hurts, even when we have to reach into our own needed substance. This is the meaning of the incident of the poor widow and her little coins, which were in fact all she had. (Mk 12:42–44).

2. We have to give when the occasion demands it, when our neighbor's need calls for it—and not when we have a comfortable excess. The needs of a neighbor or stranger are quite autonomous and independent of our own. They may present themselves in times of our own prosperity or in times of need. The Jewish Scriptures praise the widow for giving her last food to the prophet Elijah in the time of famine (1 Kings 17:1–16). In the parable of the Good Samaritan, Our Lord describes a man doing acts of kindness to a stranger in a dangerous and desolate place. How many of us would be willing to take a chance in a dangerous neighborhood to help a stranger who is obviously hurt?

[6] Schnackenburg, *Moral Teaching,* 100–101.

The charity called for by the Son of God is obviously not an ego trip. It is that special kind of love—charity or agape.

Charity: The Freeing of the Ego

It is possible that the Christian life of most of us has become boring and unfocused, even a dull burden, because we have forgotten the challenge of charity. Have we been lulled into thinking that the duty of charity is just a little extra responsibility of our life that we may or may not choose to do? The great obstacle to charity in our time is materialism. When most American Catholics were poor working people they supported a gigantic system of social agencies and schools. Now that many Catholics are middle to upper class, they do much less in proportion. As a group, Christians in the United States have been jaded by material possessions. We need to be reminded that renunciation of worldly wealth and its distribution to the poor were required by Jesus not only of the disciples who wanted to follow Him personally but also to a lesser degree of all who believed in Him (Lk 12:33).[7]

If God has given us His superabundant gift of salvation, we too must give to those who ask and must lend without expecting anything in return. And here, as with forgiveness, the motive is the love of God. We are told, however, that we shall receive in the same measure that we have been generous. This eros and agape, need and generous self-giving, are not contradictory but complementary to each other.

[7] Schnackenburg, *Moral Teaching,* 102.

Love and Reform

It is worth noting that the most powerful reform moments in the history of the Church have been linked directly to agape in its many forms. The restoration of worship, the purification of the heart, the education of the young and the ignorant, the care of the poor and the destitute—all works of agape or charity—are inevitably linked with the work of reform of the Church and society. Benedict, Bernard, Francis and Clare, Dominic, the two Catherines (of Siena and of Genoa), Ignatius, Vincent de Paul and Louise de Marillac, Francis de Sales and Chantal—this is a partial litany of those who linked love of God and neighbor to reform. Right up to this moment, if you find a true Catholic reformer, you find a person seeking to love God and neighbor without regard to personal fulfillment or need. You find those who have put their ego needs, even legitimate ones, behind them, and who strive, perhaps with only moderate success, to follow the powerful psychological insight of Saint Paul: *"Caritas Christi urget nos"* (The love of Christ impells us on) (2 Cor 5:14).

Chapter Eight

THE REFORM OF RELIGIOUS LIFE

Religious life in the United States is in a mess. A *mess* is defined by the *American Heritage Dictionary* as a "disturbing, confusing, and troublesome state of affairs. . . . Senseless confusion and discontinuity; chaos".[1] This colloquialism has been chosen not only for emphasis. The term *mess* has actually been chosen so that the author can be quoted more succinctly and accurately by friend and foe. A mess suggests many things mixed together, some good, some bad, some questionable. There are pleasant mixtures, which are often called collages if they are visual, or fugues if they are auditory. In the wealthier countries religious life is no longer a pleasant mixture; it is a mess.

Chaos and Decline

Gerald Arbuckle, the well-known anthropologist of religious life, calls the present situation chaos and suggests that the next step can be refounding and new life.[2] But he also points out that often after chaos comes death. A living

---

[1] *American Heritage Dictionary,* 2d college ed., s.v. "mess".
[2] Gerald Arbuckle, *Out of Chaos* (Boston: Houghton Mifflin, 1982; New York: Paulist Press, 1988).

thing in a mess may simply be in the ultimate stage of deterioration. The religious life is meant to be made up of dedicated people seeking to follow the highest goals of contemplative prayer, charity and generous self-giving. Religious follow a tradition that has given the human race some of its noblest and most altruistic figures. That this way of life can be described as a mess is a sign that an age of reform is again approaching.

A careful reading of Church history will reveal a paradox. One would expect that religious people would be the last holdouts in a declining society. Considering the goals of professed religious and their self-imposed discipline, one would think that when civil and ecclesiastical institutions begin to go into moral and cultural decline, the followers of such great souls as Benedict, Scholastica, Dominic, Francis, Clare and Ignatius would hold the line. And indeed, in every age of decline there have been religious who did try, usually with limited success, to keep alive the spirit of the Gospel. But for the most part, religious communities have been strangely susceptible to decline. They have usually gone down as quickly as any other institution in society. Several explanations suggest themselves. It is an observable fact of life, among plants, animals and men, that the more developed forms are the most delicate and most sensitive to change. A garden of flowers is more vulnerable to environmental change than a forest of trees; thoroughbreds are more delicate than a pack of wolves; a university faculty is more responsive to environmental change than a local of construction workers. Not infrequently more developed forms of life actually cause their own demise by becoming too removed from their original environment and consequently too vulnerable to change.

After about four decades in religious life, I am convinced

that this analogy has some validity. When I became a friar during the period of religious fervor that resulted from the Second World War, religious life was flourishing. Discipline was strict to the point of being stifling. Ideals and goals were high and, in fact, at times neurotic and somewhat unrealistic. This is well illustrated by the autobiography of Thomas Merton, *The Seven Storey Mountain*.[3] Like the majority of his contemporaries who entered religious life at that time, Merton had discovered the conflict between time and eternity, between the world and the spirit. Like millions of people before him, Merton sought to resolve the conflict in somewhat simplistic ways. He and his fellow Cistercians, along with the rest of us religious, sought to reappraise these ways in the postconciliar age beginning in the mid-1960s. The important point here is that it was in the two decades after the Second World War that the life of religious communities was characterized by a spirit of otherworldliness, of serious attempts toward personal reform and turning to that which does not change. Great works of charity and education and large-scale missionary efforts overseas and at home characterized religious life only three decades ago.

Even before the Second Vatican Council, thoughtful observers noticed a sea change. The number of applicants began to drop, while discontent with many aspects of religious life continued to increase. Psychology and sociology were invoked to find some answers. With a dogmatism characteristic of those who believe that God has promised to keep them from making any serious mistakes, religious communities uncritically put aside Tradition and discipline

[3] Thomas Merton, *The Seven Storey Mountain* (New York: Harcourt, Brace, 1948).

in favor of being relevant and keeping up with the "signs of the times". Almost all of this effort was well intentioned; much of it was paradoxically very dictatorial; little of it was critically thought through. The results, for a complex set of reasons, were disastrous. One writer who studied vocational recruitment noted a very strange phenomenon, the trend of religious communities today to deny that a disaster is taking place at all. Communities with no vocations reported that they had the best recruitment and formation programs ever. I sat at a general chapter once and listened for fifteen minutes to the glowing description of a wonderful formation program in France. The coordinators energetically did this, and novices imaginatively did that, we were told. But in a moment reality showed its terrifying head. When the speaker was asked directly, he admitted that there were no students in the program.

To be dangerously ill is bad enough, but to be unaware of the danger is perilous. To deny prelethal symptoms is plain self-destruction. Evolution will do the rest.

To the thoughtful observer of the passing scene, all of this may seem like beating a flock of dead sheep, but it is worth noting that many Catholic religious will be angered and chagrined by what I have written. Some will, inconceivably, deny the facts. They will react as did those who participated in a study of religious life in the United States that pronounced it basically sound. Others will recognize all too well that what is being described is true, but they will ask, Why hang crepe? These are people who generally like funerals to be cheery events with lots of alleluias and pleasantries. Some others will be annoyed because they have kept on giving and struggling in religious life, buoyed up by the hope that somehow or other it will all work out in the end: "If we can just hold on, there will be a better day." I used to belong to this group. I will attempt to summarize why I gave up waiting for Godot and decided to bypass the Lamentations of Jeremiah and see what Jonah the prophet had to offer in the way of a call to reform.

The Present Situation

There are several serious signs of the imminent demise of many religious communities of men or women. Perhaps the majority of communities are in the last stages of decomposition and in a decade or two will have totally disappeared. Others, especially older worldwide communities, will probably survive but with very reduced numbers and deeply shattered identities. They are actually dead, but like ancient olive trees, new life may grow out of the old roots and preserve the appearance that the tree has been living for centuries. There are indeed a few communities that are alive. They are attracting and keeping reasonable numbers of new members, and, what is more important, they have preserved their identity. They know who they are, they believe in who they are and they try to live accordingly. These are usually, but not always, smaller communities of fewer than a hundred members with a strong family spirit, traditional values and clearly defined goals and apostolates. Unfortunately, these communities are often intimidated and even laughed at. This derision causes them at times to close in on themselves in ways that are counterproductive.

A few communities of men or women have survived the storm by remaining purposely aloof from the present life of the Church. They have strong values and identity, but history has often assigned them a place that is ultraconservative, despite the fact that their founders sought in very creative ways to affect the life of the Church in their own times. The danger is that these communities may become living fossils, without meaning to do anything more than protect themselves from a whole movement in religious life that is running lemminglike into the sea.

It is necessary to point out to those less familiar with religious life that scattered around this wasteland are thousands of religious who lead devout, prayerful and dedicated lives. Among them are many older religious who admit to being heartbroken and deeply disturbed and younger religious who have learned to make it by leaning on God alone. These usually admit that things are as bad as the facts suggest. As one Franciscan bishop commented to me recently, "There are many good religious, but there is little religious life!"

Whatever else can be said of the present state of religious life, it appears to be the result of a cultural movement that has affected every religious institution in the Western nations, by either threatening to dissolve them or forcing them into an isolated existence or, as in the case of small communities, causing them to strengthen the familial ties of religious life.

The complex causes of the present crisis have been very well analyzed in the book *Strategies for Growth in Religious Life*[4] by Father Gerald Arbuckle, a Marist priest who is also a very well qualified anthropologist. Arbuckle's revealing observations in his second book, *Out of Chaos,*[5] form part of the foundation of this appeal for reform and indeed have prompted the writing of this book. We shall borrow from

[4] Gerald Arbuckle, *Strategies for Growth in Religious Life* (New York: Alba House, 1986).

[5] See n. 2 above.

his conclusions at the end of this chapter. It is sufficient to point out here that if he is correct in his assumption that religious life is going through a crisis as a result of cultural change and dislocation, it is a waste of time to try to assign blame to anyone in particular. Responsibility should have been taken by those who had some influence or authority. But this responsibility is not necessarily something for them to repent of now. Who could have foreseen where things were going? Thousands of prayerful, well-meaning persons made or participated in decisions that became part of a program for chaos. The important thing now is to appraise things realistically and make effective decisions for change. If one is living in the past, it makes no difference whether it is ten years ago or fifty years ago. Leave the past behind. It is over! Let us face realistically what is coming.

Danger Signs

While it is difficult to describe the danger signs in religious life without being tedious, it is necessary to recognize the symptoms to make adequate plans for therapy. Medical practice would supply the analogy of a general systemic infection that affects the entire functioning of the patient. Who knows whether one symptom is more dangerous than another? An attempt will be made here to identify the most dangerous symptoms, especially the most insidious. The reader may not agree with this selection and may see other signs as more alarming. The present diagnosis is based on the central theme of this book, namely, that the Christian life is a process of repentance and reform leading to renewal. If you are a priest or religious, it is suggested that you not waste your energies asking the question, Am I part of the symptom or not? Take it from me: we are all infected. We are all part of the syndrome. Ask yourself what you are doing, as part of the fabric of your community (or diocese), to cope creatively and critically with these symptoms and their causes.

Loss of Purpose: The Denial of the Vows

The vows of poverty, chastity and obedience (or whatever parallel promises are indicated in the particular legislation of a religious community) have been seen traditionally as the existential foundation of religious life. The substance of these vows is defined in Canon Law. Indeed, as the great Anglican scholar of spirituality Evelyn Underhill has observed, these vows codify in a particular way the qualities of life required of anyone who is seriously pursuing the spiritual journey.[6] Regardless of a person's state of life, avoiding materialism, sensuality and arrogant self-will is necessary for anyone seeking to come closer to God. In the Sermon on the Mount, Christ made it mandatory for all His disciples that they seriously attempt to live by the qualities which the vows entail. They are an integral part of His call for conversion. There are innumerable Christians, married and single, who live lives similar to those religious, but who never thought of taking a vow. The vowed life requires a person to declare publicly that he will seriously pursue these qualities. And in the case of religious who pursue this goal as members of an order, a strong, thriving community must provide an austere and frugal life, with supportive familial relationships, in place of marriage. The religious

---

[6] Evelyn Underhill, *Mysticism* (New York: E. P. Dutton, 1961), 205.

community must be in an environment that sustains charity and directs one's talents for the service of the kingdom of God. Since the Church's earliest days the spiritual and corporal works of mercy have been seen as an integral part of religious life. The Catholic Church has required religious to serve others by appropriate work and prayer and to be united to the whole Church through loyalty to the Bishop of Rome. In ways similar to the ordained clergy, all religious — lay or clerical — are to be public witnesses to the Gospel, which they seek to follow in their own spiritual life.

At present, every single one of the vows is being questioned as regards its usefulness, propriety, psychological possibility and form of observance. Many religious observe the vows only minimally, and many, often through no fault of their own, are deprived of the support of genuine community life. Because of serious ideological differences about basic Christian teachings, many religious live alone or in little clusters that do not resemble community life. The external, universal sign of religious life — plain, uniform garb with a recognizable sign of commitment — has been replaced by secular attire. The well-known psychological anthropologist Victor Turner has identified religious garb as one of the components of liminality. He sees liminality — the quality of being an outsider — as an essential aspect of the religious resolution of the conflict between worldly and spiritual values.[7] Many sincerely motivated young people have complained to me that they feel called to religious life but can find no community that offers them any spiritual advantages that they cannot find as lay Christians. What is more deplorable, many young people say that what they observe

---

[7] Victor Turner, *The Ritual Process* (Chicago: Aldine, 1969), 106.

going on in religious life would actually be an obstacle to their spiritual growth. Schools conducted by religious communities once provided abundant vocations drawn from students who were inspired by their teachers. Now those communities attract very few recruits. The same can be said of communities that do pastoral work. They often cull what few candidates they can find from young people who respond to vocational advertisements. If we are to be honest, we must admit that these ads portray an ideal often far removed from the reality found in the community.

The Neglect of the Apostolate

Beyond the collapse of community life there is the deplorable neglect of the apostolate. Christ not only called his followers to conversion; He also sent them out to preach the Gospel by word and example and to be witnesses. While the ranks of religious are in decline and the chosen apostolic works of the communities are vastly understaffed, one finds religious engaged in all kinds of work that contribute nothing to the apostolate. As one major superior put it, "We have become countersigns to the Gospel." Catholic education and identity are approaching a crisis moment in America. Catholic hospitals are already on their way to total secularization. The poor who received so much spiritual and material help from religious orders a decade or two ago are all but forgotten, except by dedicated little groups of religious who are now growing older. These religious often get little real support from their communities.

There are exceptions to all of this, thank God. But as large numbers of religious strive for some kind of self-actualization, living an upper-middle-class life-style, the poor in very large numbers are neglected, even in predominantly Catholic areas. If you are one of the religious still at work in a real apostolate, do not become angry at these statements. But ask the question a very fine religious sister who belongs to a community founded for the care of the poor asked me: "What in the world are we religious doing?"

The Betrayal of the Church

We have already discussed the theological conflict in the Church. It is regrettable but true that much of the conflict arises in the ranks of religious and is disseminated by them. Church history reveals that this has often been the case when religious life went into decline. It is not difficult to picture someone entering religious life with generosity, discipline and a sincere desire to serve God and seek personal holiness and later coming to a point of spiritual self-destruction. When all the promises fade away and when the leadership is weak and confused or even corrupt, a person of a theological cast of mind may express this disappointment by an adolescent tearing down of the very ideals that once were attractive. This is not so different from a disappointed married person's unconsciously destroying the family he founded. In both cases it is the children who suffer the most. The religious whose chosen vocation is to teach the Catholic Faith can end up undermining that Faith in students and at the same time commit a grave injustice to the parents who sacrificed much to provide what they thought would be a solid religious education. I personally know a number of teaching religious who rarely attend the liturgy or pray. It is foolish to expect that their teaching or demeanor around the students will in any way reflect the Gospel of Jesus Christ or the spirit of their founder.

Scandal and Bad Example

This brings us to the worst of dangers, namely, that religious life will provide the occasion for a person not to be a Christian at all. The literature of the Renaissance and the history of the Church on the eve of the French Revolution provide sad but pointed examples of how bad things can get in religious life. Among college students in large urban areas, among many of the clergy and among educators and professional people associated with religious institutions, it is no secret that examples of serious scandal occur all too frequently. Small but vocal groups of religious publicly attack the Church's teaching on sexual morality, homosexual behavior, abortion and other critical issues. Some of the worst expressions of disloyalty to the Holy Father or to the Church herself are voiced by religious in private, or even in public when they are not likely to be quoted. Those who claim that they are unaware of these things live either in blessed isolation, usually provided by advanced age, or on a sustained level of denial that may be seriously culpable.

The Response of the Bishops

Many bishops are profoundly concerned by the collapse of an essential arm of the Church's apostolate, namely, religious life. They are often unable to express this alarm in public for fear of damaging further the sinking morale of existing communities, especially those that are holding on to some apostolate and Tradition. The bishops are also very sensitive to the feelings of the large number of devoted, hardworking religious who remain loyal despite the confu-

sion and secularization of their communities. But it has
been my experience that many bishops, in private personal
conversation, will express profound concern and, if they
are diocesan bishops, frustration at the precarious position
of religious communities. Because of the hierarchy's fear
of hurting what survivors are left, a very strange and
more confusing phenomenon occurs. It frequently happens that the communities that are most loyal to the
Church and most observant of their common commit-
ments and that have a strong internal identity are treated
as second-class citizens and made to feel inferior by the
officials of the very Church they serve. One would expect
them to receive at least equal attention to that given those
who are publicly less supportive of the Holy Father and less
than enthusiastic (to put it mildly) about the teaching of
the Magisterium.

The Real Way Out: Conversion and Reform

While I may not be as sanguine as Father Arbuckle, who
sees this as a moment of great opportunity for religious life,
I must agree with him that individual personal conversion is
the beginning of a way out of the present confusion. He
borrows the powerful analogy of Thomas Merton concerning the cargo cults that flourished in primitive areas of New
Guinea after the first missionaries and developers arrived
with machines and electrical gadgets at the end of the
Second World War.[8] The native people labored to make

[8] Thomas Merton, "Cargo Cults in the South Pacific", *America*,
Sept. 3, 1977, p. 96.

scale models of things such as refrigerators and then went out to see if the models had been able to produce cold beer and ice. They had made what looked like exact replicas, but they had no power source. Arbuckle cites Merton's comparison of these vain endeavors to many of the changes by religious orders made after Vatican II.[9] The changed institutions looked fine from the outside, but they consistently lacked the essential energy source needed for personal conversion and spiritual goals. And so they have not produced works of the spirit. One discouraged religious sister, who has kept her sense of humor in the middle of all of this, has described many of these religious adventures that led to disaster as rearranging the deck chairs on the *Titanic* to get a better view. The idea of personal conversion was all but buried under a mound of poorly thought out psychology, naïveté, secularism and a peculiar kind of self-indulgence. This kind of behavior is to be expected when those involved in repression see through this defense mechanism and substitute in its place denial and regression. Frequently a person who escapes from repression will regress or go back to behavior that is immature. It is not unusual to observe religious who prematurely "died to themselves" by repression at eighteen rising from the dead at thirty-six—only to act as if they are eighteen again.

Personal conversion or, as we have called it in this book, an ongoing spirit of repentance and reform, will easily put religious persons into conflict with their surroundings. Under these circumstances prayer will become an absolute necessity. This prayer will not involve some nice psychological exercise of self-satisfaction and self-hypnotism. It will be painful, disturbing prayer that will call for soul-searching and change.

[9] Arbuckle, *Strategies,* 118–20.

It will require honesty and force those who remain faithful to the unpleasant conclusion that they must think, speak and act differently. In real prayer we discover more and more the holiness of God and our failure to make real decisions of life in His favor. Prayer reveals our self-seeking, our subtle narcissism and our vices all wrapped up in nice pleasantries. But do not turn away from this conflict. If you are a religious and you really pray and change, you provide hope for your community to be reformed and renewed.

Father Arbuckle has some excellent advice for those in charge of religious communities as to how they can assist their groups in a process he called refounding, literally, starting over again. He makes the obvious point that it is best if a community can be refounded from within rather than starting a new community on the same foundation and expressing the same values as the founder. But refounding requires brave and honest people in positions of authority and a general agreement that reform is necessary. In a word, it requires people who are willing to admit that they need constant personal and communal reform.[10]

Unfortunately, very few communities are actually prepared for something as radical as refounding. Religious— even very good religious—get so involved in existential personal considerations that the thought of another change is appalling. The conflicts involved, the personal sacrifices, the restoration of discipline, which was once seen as repression for repression's sake, all of these coupled with the uncertainty of the enterprise cause even well-meaning religious to assume a passive attitude. This attitude will bring their sick community to a peaceful death. There are also those who are completely opposed to reform because of

[10] Arbuckle, *Out of Chaos*, chaps. 5 and 6.

various abuses to which they have become all too accustomed. If one takes the warnings of the Gospel seriously, these religious urgently need prayer. The awesome paintings of the pre-Reformation period showing foolish and worldly religious on their way to perdition can certainly be a warning to those religious who at this time are unwilling to change because of the fear of their own discomfort.

Reform: Vital and Spontaneous

Only when the spirit of reform has begun to develop will the genuine practical dimensions of change begin to appear. The process is spontaneous, vital and though at times controversial, its feeling is totally different from the heady and overdebated processes of change religious have experienced in the past twenty years. Refounding is altogether different. Something new is experienced. I have had this personal experience.

A small group of religious joined together by prayer and common evangelical purpose, enthusiastic with the spirit of the founder and of loyalty to the Church, does not need a lot of help from visiting psychologists, sociologists or even theologians. Theory, though important, is not as important as it was in the past two decades, when religious communities searched everywhere to find a new identity. Having experienced the vital force of a group of people drawn together for a common purpose, willing to risk their good names and futures and strengthened in their loyalty to one another by the criticism they encountered, I am convinced that refounding can only be a painful but thrilling experience. It is worth enduring a lot of conflict simply to be delivered from the barrage of ideas that can never be trusted and from the doldrums of hearing all the reasons why good things cannot be done.

Apostolic and Loyal

As in all works of the apostolate, refounding must certainly be guided by the Church and especially by her highest authority, the Pope. There must be a conviction of the validity of the Church's claim to be the vehicle of salvation and sacramental life established by Christ. This conviction leads to loyalty to the Church even in the worst of circumstances.

Religious interested in refounding must be guided by bishops who themselves experience the need for reform. Saint Francis ordered the friars not to remain in the diocese of any bishop opposed to them and the reform they represented. This is still wise advice.

Commitment to God's Will

Beyond all of this, however, there must be the conviction on the part of each religious that the pursuit of such a perilous task is God's will. They may arrive at such a conclusion in a variety of ways. One person may be passionately devoted to the ideals of the founder and find it impossible to live with an official presentation of them that can only be termed mediocre, if one is very kind. Another may have a great loyalty to the Church and wish to do something effective to assist the Church in this time of crisis. Another may have a simple devotion to Our Lord and be unwilling to endure His name's being used to bless vain and worldly pursuits. Another may find the whole present scene grossly irreverent, an unendurable affront to God. Yet another may see a call to reform as a simple moral obligation coming from the Commandments and the Sermon on the Mount. To do otherwise would be to commit a grave sin. A number of people interested in reform and refounding may have several different motives at the same time.

No one but a saint will have pure motives. Less worthy motives that are likely to be mixed in include frustration, anger, self-righteousness, hurt feelings and the like. These inadequate motives will be quickly pointed out by religious opposed to reform or by those who think about it in the abstract but are unable, for one reason or another, to do anything practical. The would-be reformer must be willing constantly to learn from critics. We learn a great deal from our critics once we have removed any poison from the criticism by prayer. And, strangely, in religious life the axiom is true that the best things that are said about people are said about them by their enemies. No one, especially a religious, should even utter the word *reform* without prayerful meditation on the words of Christ: "How blest are you when men revile you and say all manner of things against you. Be glad and rejoice for your reward will be great in heaven" (Mt 5:11–12).

Religious Life Will Survive and Lead Again

Religious life has existed wherever and whenever the Church has existed. It has already been observed that it is vulnerable to change and very susceptible to decline and even corruption. But in its roots it is also very hearty and difficult to kill. Religious life often comes back from the dead.

The history of religious life reveals that when it comes back to life through reform, the reformers look little like today's liberals or conservatives. As we have mentioned, these words are so abused at present as to be almost useless, except to identify rather complex masses of people held together by certain rather poorly thought out ways of responding. Because of their links with Tradition, the so-called conservatives often have much more identity, but they need to be converted like everybody else. The liberals, in contrast, may be more open to change and consequently to the idea of reform.

Regardless of what you think you are, if you are a religious and you call yourself a liberal or a conservative or a middle-of-the-roader (the most elusive of identities), what do you make of the possibility of reform? It is not necessary to repeat all that has been said previously in this book about reform. How do you apply it to yourself? Would any young person looking at your life be inspired by your personal poverty? Would he be drawn by your chaste love of others? Would he see you as one who seeks to do the will of God? What would he think of your community? Would he see it as supporting you in fervent prayer, apostolic work and love for the spiritually and physically needy? If the answer to these questions is no or maybe, the time for you to ask yourself about reform is now.

Chapter Nine

REFORM IN THE CLERGY

Generalizations about the life of the clergy in any given society, whether of a single religion or of several faiths and denominations, are likely to be misleading. At any moment there are surely to be found among the clergy saints and sinners, the gifted and people of moderate and even mediocre talents, the devout and the worldly. Many psychosocial studies and evaluations have been done on the clergy in the past two decades. Unfortunately, the possibility of making misleading judgments about the American clergy based on these studies is paradoxically much greater than it was without them, because many, including church leaders, were not prepared to evaluate such studies critically or to assess the degree of probability or, more frequently, the degree of improbability of the conclusions drawn.

A Personal Note

Because of my own interest in such studies and because of the damage done by imposing conclusions that were based on very flimsy data, I would rather write about the spiritual condition of the clergy on the basis of fifteen years' experience with Catholic clergy and with Protestant and Jewish clergy as well. This experience includes teaching, conducting workshops and providing spiritual direction, counseling and, occasionally, psychotherapy. Most of this experience was in the New York area, but it included many trips around the country and overseas. I have been called upon to assist several hundred priests who left the active ministry, and I have enjoyed assisting over forty-five priests to return. In my work as counselor to the clergy, I have been involved with priests, deacons, seminarians and religious brothers. I have been called upon to offer some assistance to Orthodox clergy, High Church Episcopalians, Lutherans, Evangelicals and Fundamentalists, mainstream Protestants, clergy of liberal denominations, several rabbis, a few women clergy and a fascinating assortment of Mormons, Adventists and, once, a Buddhist monk.

The Root of the Problem

I would hazard a guess that the root of the problem of the clergy in the United States is that up to now we have had it too easy. A century and a half ago, de Tocqueville observed of the United States that "religion was all over the place". Unlike the clergy in most European countries and in Asia, American clergy have never been through a period of persecution. Catholic and Jewish clergy have, with their laity, endured religious prejudice, but it was not what one would call persecution. Not so long ago, in the postwar era, the clergy probably enjoyed as much respect in America and in much of Europe as they ever have.

A Change in the Climate

Now the media have obviously turned on the clergy and enjoy attacking them. On television, in popular novels and in various kinds of muckraking the clergy are experiencing harassment and criticism unparalleled in American life. This follows right along with the European media, although in the United States it is more coarse, with sacrilegious humor and sensational coverage of the moral failures of individual clergy. Catholic and Evangelical Protestant clergy are special targets of the media because they are generally the only clergy who take issue with particular causes that those in the media support. The position of the Catholic clergy, most of the Evangelical ministers and the Orthodox Jews on issues such as abortion, public approval of homosexual life-styles and the sexual revolution make them the target of abuse with which no other profession in American life has to put up. Along with the hostility of the media, the general decline of religious activity, the continued secularization of culture and the movement of Catholic ethnic groups up the social and economic ladder, there have been a predictable loss of vocations and withdrawals from the ordained clergy.

These facts, which negatively affect the priesthood and represent the first large-scale reversal of the popular acceptance of the clergy in America, unfortunately are not the kind of adversity that produces positive results. If the clergy in the past were too well accepted, it might seem logical that this reversal of opinion would now help the growth and identity of the clergy, as is happening in Latin America. There, for the first time in hundreds of years, the clergy in all ranks find themselves at odds with governments and the powerful. The result is the first large-scale popular movement into the clergy since the discovery of America.

What is happening in the United States and Europe at present is not this kind of rejection that inspires the young, clears out the deadwood and elicits heroic stands in the face of evil. In North America the Catholic clergy and much of the Protestant clergy are being dismissed as irrelevant, anachronistic and often unsure of their own identity. This is even more true of many religious. The religious history of France reveals that this kind of opposition and the clergy's often intimidated response do not help the Church. Whereas the French Revolution and the waves of persecution that followed it occasioned a huge number of priestly and religious vocations and an unparalleled missionary outreach, the skepticism and religious cynicism of the 1960s and 1970s have had the opposite effect in America and much of Europe.

Losing Ground

What is happening in the United States, it seems to this author, is the depletion of spiritual and even material resources. The past immense popularity of the clergy, the respect that existed for religious, the gigantic resources for good that had been accumulated by dioceses and orders during decades of dedicated toil, are being used up at an alarming rate. I was one of those who strongly disagreed with the prophets of doom in the 1960s. They said that religious communities were going to die before they could come back to life. I agreed with those who believed that it was merely a difficult period of transition and that some bright morning we would all wake up and there would be a renewal of vocations to put spark back into the solid religious orders and institutions that had survived. Perhaps this might have happened if religious orders had not lost their nerve at that time. Who knows?

The case with the diocesan clergy is different. The diocesan clergy simply cannot die out, as religious orders do. Somehow, somewhere, even in the worst of times, the Church and her basic clergy survive.

But now questions such as the following are being asked. Can the celibate priesthood survive? Can we adequately serve the Church without permitting married men to be ordained or priests to marry? A subject that has its roots in an entirely different phenomenon, but is obviously involved, is the changing role of women and ultimately of men. The desire of women to have what is seen as full equality raises the question of women's ordination, something obviously at odds with the Tradition of the Church, since it has never happened before.

The question of women's ordination would have arisen anyway, but urgency is added to it because of the decline of vocations resulting from the indifference and apathy of men. The Episcopal church, which actually went against its tradition when it ordained women, has the anomalous situation of having too many clergy and too few laity. The change to permit the ordination of women has filled the pulpits but not the pews.

The Easy Answer

The quick and easy answer to the problem of shortages of vocations to the priesthood has been to relax clerical discipline. This answer, was almost universally adopted to some degree because so many standards in American life became flexible, if not completely arbitrary. From clothing styles to sexual morality, the Western world moved in two decades from a rather refined and idealistic set of mores to a world without heroes and almost without mores of any kind at all. From clothing styles, which are usually harmless and arbitrary, to sexual morality, which affects the very fabric of society, everything changed. In the Western world and even the Eastern bloc, there has been a continual movement toward moral relaxation and fewer personal demands. The trend has been simply to make things easier for people. The crucial question has become: Is it easy to do good or to do ill, to be helpful or to be self-indulgent? Expectations of the clergy relaxed, as they did for all other professional groups, except in a very limited way for those in the areas of academic and professional preparation. Ease in general has been the rule of the last two decades.

New Influences on the Clergy

Because of this very great relaxation, changes were made in the training of the clergy. Academics churned out arguments that brought many beliefs and moral convictions into question. Psychology—and to a lesser extent sociology— became the focus of these questions and often demolished the old human values without replacing them with anything except a mindless belief that human nature, left unhampered and without responsibility, would find the way. An incipient Pelagianism, which had its roots more recently in Rousseau's idea of the perfect natural man, became the religious philosophy of many, despite its obvious incompatibility with several major Christian beliefs, including original sin and redemption. The brave new world of relaxed standards and discarded values was uncritically accepted by vast numbers of educated Christians, including many clergy and religious. Carl Rogers replaced Saint Augustine; Sigmund Freud was taken completely out of his deeply pessimistic context and made the apostle of a freedom that he did not believe existed. In Scripture, systematic theology and moral theology, ideas were taken from nineteenth-century rationalism and positivism and presented to seminarians and Catholic college students as consistent with Christianity. American public education, which has always been optimistic and idealistic, passed into this brave new world without as much as a look back. Educators assumed that human nature, left on its own without any education in values or any repression, would come spontaneously, even magically, to some new level of human development. None of this, of course, actually happened.

One of the first people to see the danger signs was the president of the American Psychological Association, Professor Donald Campbell. In his presidential address to the American Psychological Association in 1975 he criticized the American educational system for undermining the moral fabric of our society.[1]

Right behind Campbell came several social scientists. Christopher Lasch, of the University of Rochester, saw Americans moving not toward an age of new freedom but rather toward an age of destructive narcissism.[2] A decade later Daniel Yankelovich, of New York University, did an autopsy on selfism, a value system that puts the self first. He believed that young people would move beyond selfism

---

[1] As cited in Paul Vitz, *Psychology as Religion* (Grand Rapids, Mich.: Eerdmans, 1975), 49.

[2] Christopher Lasch, *The Culture of Narcissism* (New York: W. W. Norton Co., 1979).

because it is ultimately self-destructive and isolated.[3] His book can be used as an argument for the natural law.

Paradoxically, these writers all began from a secular perspective. They did not claim to have religious values, much less specifically Christian ones. Here it would be helpful for us to remember that children of this world can be wiser in their own generation than the children of the light.

For twenty years Christians of almost every denomination—and certainly of all segments of American Catholicism—have been busy trying to incorporate or, if you will, baptize psychosocial theories that are essentially at odds with their basic beliefs. The result is a house sadly divided. Christians are still so busy working on baptizing selfism that they have failed to recognize what Yankelovich has pointed out, namely, that selfism as a practical guide in life leaves a person desperately isolated, without any real values and without hope. Yankelovich even predicted that fairly large numbers of young adults would become so horrified by this solipsism that they would move back toward the old values of self-giving and altruism.

Selfism and the Clergy

What has selfism to do with the reform of the American clergy? Simply everything! Pastoral people—clergy, active religious and dedicated lay workers—are among the most culturally sensitive groups in America. When everyone realized the value of psychological testing for career planning,

[3] Daniel Yankelovich, *New Rules* (New York: Random House, 1981).

clergy and religious became the most tested segment of the population. When many clamored for renewal, the clergy and religious were the most renewed. And so the clergy—especially the Catholic clergy—have been studied, tested and reshaped; preached to, confronted and renewed. Priests, seminarians and religious, more than any other people I can think of, have been exposed to the most violent winds of cultural change. This process has left them not only a bit unsteady but also unaware that the ideas presented to them were often contradictory. Sometimes these ideas were intellectually and even morally inconsistent with their professed religious beliefs. Not lacking on both the liberal and conservative sides were bishops and leaders who wondered if all this new thinking could be digested as fast as it was presented. Some very hardy souls even questioned whether some of it was consistent with the basic beliefs of Christianity and the Tradition of the Church. Psychologists and psychiatrists involved in therapy with clergy and religious often wondered if the simple rapidity of the changes and their scope left many people disoriented. Many married Catholics concerned with raising families and other down-to-earth considerations wondered whether all the discussion was really necessary.

The Man in the Middle

The person caught in the middle of all this turmoil in the Catholic Church was the priest doing pastoral work, whether he was diocesan or religious. The person next in line was the seminarian and potential candidate who felt called to take his place in the clergy.

The responses of priests have varied, of course. Some,

especially older priests, decided to plead the clerical fifth amendment, to comply with what was necessary, such as liturgical norms and such structural changes as parish councils, and then wait out the storm. Without a strong theological foundation younger clergy could not do this so easily. Many went along, trying diligently to keep up with and integrate the new ideas that they had been taught. A great many of these priests left the priesthood in an intellectual and emotional vertigo that forced them to step back to preserve their basic emotional stability.

My experience with priests strongly suggests that the rapidity of change was the largest single cause for many to leave the priesthood. Others moved in the opposite direction, becoming more traditional and—to use a popular term— more conservative. They tended to reject much of the new because they saw how confusing it was to those who embraced "the new Church". Finally, some others began to lead a double life. The positive value of pastoral work— helping others, acceptance and gratitude—kept men actively in the ministry but spiritually out of the priesthood. The disturbing novel by Miguel de Unamuno about a dedicated priest who does not believe in God began to have prophetic significance.[4] There were cases of hardworking priests who admitted to having families clandestinely, and then resigned. Many others who left provided proof of one of the more obvious facts of psychological anthropology, that religiously motivated celibacy can exist only when there is a strong commitment to orthodox religious belief.

---

[4] Miguel de Unamuno, "Saint Manuel Bueno, Martyr", in *Spanish Stories and Tales,* ed. H. de Oris (New York: Alfred A. Knopf, 1954).

The Present: Confusion Becomes Apathy and Cynicism

The present situation not only among the clergy but also among religious and the laity suggests that there is a growing sense of apathy spreading through the Church. This is particularly noticeable in northern Europe, where the changes have come with greater force than they did in America. But the apathy grows in America, too. Priests are tired. Conscientious priests are overworked and receive insufficient reinforcement from the laity. The world goes on without them and puts less and less value on their ministry, except for such rites of passage as required by birth, marriage and death. The moral teachings of the Church are so much at odds with the prevailing mores that often priests are too intimidated to preach about personal sin and the need for confession and repentance. Bishops faced with the apathy try to use various techniques to keep up morale. By reason of the common pressures that all clergy feel, bishops tend to be closer now to priests than they had been in the past, and we can be thankful that there is a growing interdependence and a sense of sharing in many dioceses and religious communities. This is one positive sign in the whole situation.

Beyond apathy, there is a much more serious problem, and that is a growing cynicism. Cynicism has always been an underlying problem of the Christian clergy, because cynics are disappointed idealists. When the clergy are recruited from among the very young and idealistic, there is always a possibility of cynicism when the ideals of youth wear off. When the leaders and teachers of religious faith begin to show signs of confusion and hesitancy, when they sound an uncertain trumpet, who will follow? When there is a diminishing positive response to the clergy and to its ministry, then cynicism is increased by a growing belief that one has been duped by God.

According to several friends of mine who work primarily with priests, cynicism is the largest challenge facing the clergy right now. Cynicism is also observable in the Protestant clergy. Among Catholic clergy, however, celibacy and the concomitant frustration of sexual desire (especially when the value of celibacy is in question) can become extremely demoralizing and fuel the fires of cynicism. Chaste celibacy requires not only commitment but also appreciation of its value.

A Dangerous Alternative: Careerism

One way out of this cynicism is damaging and ultimately unproductive, but it provides a dangerous short-term answer. This answer is careerism. The clergy, even religious clergy, have always had career ladders. They are not always bad. In fact, clergy in career work have often done great good. The career ladder was usually well disguised because self-seeking and ambition are obviously contrary to the teaching of Christ in the Gospel and to other New Testament writers. This is true despite the fact that Saint Paul is often quoted out of context on the desirability of becoming a bishop. *Careerism* as I am using the term pejoratively means selecting a position or role in the clergy that one is going to pursue at all costs. It refers not only to the obvious ecclesiastical ladder of success but also to a myriad of side functions. Men have sold their souls to become assistant directors of the diocesan Cub Scouts or Brownies. Religious have sold out for even less—I suspect that sometime in Church history someone has committed murder to become assistant bell ringer of a monastery.

Careerism can include all sorts of other professions ancillary to the priesthood itself, such as teaching, writing, practicing psychology and so on. Actually, there is nothing intrinsically wrong with a priest's having a career, but it has its dangers. If necessary for his vocation how easily will he give up this secondary role? How much of his apostolate will be sacrificed for it? Will it substitute for his spiritual life and curtail necessary personal relationships? Careers of every sort can become worldly goals that stand in the way of the kingdom of God.

Whatever else can be said about careers in the priesthood and religious life, they are not long-term solutions to apathy or cynicism. Ultimately in Christianity and especially in a celibate priesthood with its responsibility for obedience to authority, no career can ever provide a lasting substitute for the true motive of love of God and neighbor. It is said of Cardinal Wolsey, that eminent careerist, that he summed it up so well as he ended his life in disgrace by proclaiming that he had not served God as well as his King. Thomas More, in contrast, had been willing to lay aside an eminent career because he had consistently put the service of God first in his life.

The New Clergy: Deacons and Pastoral Workers

The word *cleric* means someone set aside for the service of God. In the Catholic Church there is a growing new clergy— the permanent deacons. When the diaconate was restored as a permanent part of the clergy, there was some real question because these deacons, for the most part, would continue to live and work in the secular community, and as family men they would not be in most senses of the word set apart.

Deacons would be theologically clergy and anthropologically laity.

It is the opinion of this writer that when the diaconate preparation and training have been good, deacons have proven to be of tremendous assistance to bishops and priests, especially when there is a shortage of priests. Those opposed to the celibacy of the priesthood, as well as those in favor of the ordination of women, have generally been critical of the diaconate because paradoxically they see it as possibly saving the celibate presbyterate. These militant anticlericals are hoping that the shortage of priests gets worse. In some cases they are even working for this by discouraging seminarians and potential candidates to the celibate priesthood. Deacons, in contrast, are generally recruited from devout and moderately traditional Catholics. The deacons are easy but not fair game for these militants, because they usually are not in a position to fight back. From my years of experience with the diaconate, I have concluded that most of the time the deacons do not even recognize the real reason they are being attacked—namely, because they are a factor in preserving the celibate priesthood.

In the broadest anthropological use of the term, even other people represent a kind of new clergy. There are an assortment of laypeople and religious who now can take part in various ministerial and pastoral roles, especially by reading at the liturgy and bringing the Eucharist to the sick. (Now all you clerical elitists, calm down! I know that they are not *real* clergy. God forbid! They are too devout!)

It is not fair to call any of these people, beginning with the permanent deacons, to clerical reform. These ministries are simply too new to need reform. Everyone involved in these ministries, of course, needs to hear the general call to personal reform and repentance about which we are speaking in this book. The ministries themselves are in the process of developing and indeed need constant enrichment and reshaping.

There is one point, however, that needs to be made. These ministries came into being at a time when there was a real danger of and trend toward narcissism, self-adulation and ultrapersonalism in liturgical life. One hopes that the narcissistic liturgical carnival will soon be over. It has been a flop in the estimation of many people. These lay ministers ought to go individually into a quiet corner and examine their own participation in the liturgy to see if it has become a show for the fans. They ought to examine their own lives on precisely the issues raised here for priests and bishops. Do they pray? Are they generous? Are they examples of Christian modesty and unworldliness? Are they loyal to the Church? Are they witnesses to Christian values in a hedonistic culture? I believe that the new ministries are going to be one of the most effective and lasting benefits of the Vatican Council. But they will be effective only if those who share these ministries are constantly growing as disciples of Christ.

Reform and the Average Member of the Clergy

The focus of this book is not the shortage of vocations and the problems of the Church. It is the reform of the lives of those who have accepted a vocation or who perhaps are called to accept one. The obvious questions become: What is the condition of the clergy? Do they need reform? Many of the people reading this chapter probably consider themselves average clergy. Some readers may be bishops and leaders, some "movers and shakers", and some may style themselves conservatives, liberals or middle-of-the-roaders. Practically none of my readers may see themselves as prophetic types, and few may feel that they have either an opportunity or a responsibility to move people much outside the ordinary contacts of everyday life. All of this may be modest and accurate enough. In ordinary times they would even be correct about their responsibility. But these are not ordinary times. No one honestly thinks they are. Religion in general and the Catholic Church, along with the mainstream Protestant denominations, are losing ground rapidly. What is to be done? Most serious-minded clergy want to do something. They want to use their brief moment of life to make their providentially assigned contribution and leave the world a somewhat better place, but they need a place to start.

The place to start is definitely with one's own life. "What comes out of the mouth proceeds from the heart" (Mt 15:18). Our Savior makes it clear that what we do flows from what we are. If we are struggling for interior justice and honesty in our own hearts, we will discover in prayer and work what we need to do next. Our direction will be clearer and more creative than anything we could learn at any course or workshop or through any reading that we might do.

The Greatest Obstacle: Fear

The greatest obstacle to our doing our appointed task as disciples of Christ is fear. Like the man in the parable of the talents, we are afraid to take a risk. We are afraid of what our colleagues might say. Many of our colleagues might agree about the need for reform, but if they are all as afraid as we are, none of us will ever know that we all saw the same need. Fear of what others might think makes us all spectators, indeed, dishonest spectators, as in the story called "The Emperor's New Clothes". Fear of the multitude is an old problem of the clergy. Fear pushed Aaron and his clergy into making the golden calf while the Almighty was thundering over their shoulders. Fear drove the apostles out of Gethsemane and into little rat holes when the Son of God needed them the most. Fear and human respect are burdens for us all. Prayer—honest, silent, personal, confrontational prayer—is the only way out. The clergy need to pray for the gifts of the Holy Spirit, especially wisdom and courage, to do the great task required of them now. From bishop to priest to deacon, the clergy need to put aside self-seeking, human respect and fear of disapproval. We learn from the Gospels that the first Christian clergy really had no courage until they had seen the Lord risen from the dead and had been filled with the Holy Spirit. The only way that we can have this experience now is by personal prayer. Then we would be transformed as we see Peter and the others transformed in the Acts of the Apostles. The very thing that keeps us from such effective and powerful prayer is the fear that it actually might transform us.

Non-Catholic Clergy

This writer has been hesitant to comment in this book on the situation of non-Catholic clergy. However, it must be obvious that the same challenges that face clergy of one faith in a pluralistic and religiously diverse nation will confront most of the other clergy as well. There are in every denomination many clergy who have managed, as many Catholic priests have done, to stand apart from the tide of secularism and materialism. There are many others who have been drawn into the tide but who at least manage to preserve their basic integrity. They may recognize a need to change.

Evangelical Protestants, who often easily separated themselves from national trends, believed that their clergy were immune to the dangers of materialism and were free from worldliness and excessive interest in material gain. The scandals that have rocked the world of television evangelism and the obvious affluence sported by some of the television preachers who have survived these scandals suggest that Evangelical Protestants are no more immune than anyone else. Some of America's truly admirable evangelists such as Billy Graham have often warned that self-righteousness is never a substitute for real virtue.

It is the impression of this author that all clergy in America and, indeed, in the Western countries need to make a thorough examination of conscience. I ask myself frequently and painfully if I am actually leading a life of repentance and reform as demanded by Christ in the Gospel. Renewal was not so difficult. It could and often was done as a very human enterprise, even when accompanied by prayer. But reform can be genuinely done only with the grace of God and guided by the Holy Spirit. Repentance requires painful self-searching and constant change. The following words of Saint Augustine, quoted recently by Pope John Paul II, should be taken seriously by all clergy:

> Let your present state always leave you dissatisfied if you want to become what you are not yet. For wherever you feel satisfaction then you will stop. Say that it "is enough", you are lost. You must always look for more, look beyond, make progress.[5]

[5] Sermon 169, 18, quoted in Michael Cardinal Pelegrino, *Live What You Command* (New York: Catholic Book Publishing Co., 1975), 58.

What Is to Be Done?

It will come as no surprise to the reader that the conclusion of this author is that diocesan and religious clergy, as well as the seminarians who hope to join them, must build their daily lives on the Gospel call to repentance and reform. Perhaps the best place to begin is in a prayerful engagement of Sacred Scripture. I use the word *engagement* to avoid such words as *reading* or *studying.* In recent years there has been such a wealth of information available about the linguistics, history and social settings of the Scriptures, as well as such a plethora of theories about their composition, that the essential function of this great gift of God to man has been eclipsed. If the word of God does not lead us to personal repentance, we are not responding adequately to the admonition, "Repent, and believe the Good News" (Mk 1:15). For no group should the word of God have greater significance and accomplish more effective change than for those who are ordained to preach and teach it. There are saints who never even read the word of God, because they could not read, but the hearing of this word deeply changed their lives. Some modern scholars who have been students of the biblical writings (which are not Sacred Scripture to them) were complete unbelievers, for example, Alfred Loisy, the founder of modernism, and the late Norman Perrin, whose books are often required reading for Catholic undergraduates and who was an ex-Christian minister and an admitted unbeliever. If one wishes to avoid the warning Saint Francis gave to those who studied Scripture without attempting to respond to it wholeheartedly, then one must read it as addressed to oneself and not in some pretentious objectification that precludes any real personal response. Such things as scientific reports, cookbooks and legal and plumbing manuals can be read objectively without any personal response, although even then, there is always some subjective element in perception. But in works of social criticism, literature, philosophy, theology and most of all in the reading of the word of God, there must be a personal subjective engagement and response. Perhaps we clergy are letting God's word return to Him void.

Personal Prayer

Of the Son of God it is reported that He went into the mountains and the deserts to pray. Can anyone be ordained in His name to serve His people and ignore the obligation to pray, or can his prayer be only a slipshod and perfunctory exercise? One day a priest friend of mine was reciting the daily prayer of the Church in his office in a little corner of the ecclesiastical bureaucracy. While he was concentrating on the midday prayer of the Liturgy of the Hours, which is the official prayer of the Church, he was accosted by a clerical associate who derided him for this "pious practice". The mocking cleric ignored the fact that the Liturgy of the Hours is an obligation for priests and is also extremely beneficial for the personal spirituality of any Christian. The question was asked, "Do you still read that thing?" in the same tone that one might use to ask, Do you still believe in Santa Claus? The episode is a sad commentary on what has happened to prayer in the lives of so many of the clergy.

In his powerful book *Sensing Your Hidden Presence*, Ignacio Larranaga makes the obligation to pray very clear.[6] He points out that if you pray little, you will soon pray less, and if you pray often, you will pray better. Nothing would do the churches more good in every aspect than to have the clergy and religious begin to pray more sincerely, more reverently and more frequently.

The central act of prayer and worship for Catholics and for some other Christian churches is the liturgy of the Holy Eucharist, or the Mass. In the past two decades an immense amount of work has been done to bring the liturgy into the vernacular and to make it more personally meaningful and theologically informative. While much good has been accomplished, much is left to be desired. Recently an outstanding Benedictine educator who had been involved in liturgical reform over the years confided to me that unfortunately much of what passed for liturgical reform had declined into a narcissistic opportunity for the celebrant to be theatrical and to inspire adulation. Not to be outdone in theatrics, many persons in helping functions at the liturgy have competed with the celebrant in getting attention and winning praise.

Like sexual problems, liturgical narcissism may be another sign of the Church's need of reform. One has only to look at the funereal effigies of the English bishops immediately before the Reformation to see that they were decked with liturgical splendor and finery that distracted from and even contradicted the purpose of the liturgy, which is the worship of God. Not only Calvin and Knox but also Ignatius Loyola and John of the Cross would be less than thrilled by clown liturgies and other flamboyant exhibitions that make

---

[6] Ignacio Larranaga, O.F.M.Cap., *Sensing Your Hidden Presence: Toward Intimacy with God* (New York: Doubleday, 1987).

a personal involvement in liturgical prayer all but impossible. The center of the liturgy is the worship of God in union with Christ, the High Priest. The most appropriate human responses to such an event are reverence, devotion, devout attention and intelligent participation. While there is a deep symbolic and numinous quality to any liturgical action, it is not mere theater. There is no substitute for reverence. And conversely, there is no excuse for irreverence. A good case could be made for the observation of a friend of mine who is a university professor and dedicated layman: "Liturgical renewal has taken place. Now we need liturgical reform." Such reform cannot be accomplished by courses and workshops. It can only be accomplished when those who lead or participate in the liturgy are working on their own personal spiritual reform and life of prayer.

Simplicity and Generosity

The Epistle of Saint James identifies pure and unspoiled religion as caring for the widow and the orphan in their need and keeping oneself uncontaminated by the world (James 1:27). It has already been suggested in this book that the vulnerability of the clergy to worldliness may be an accidental result of our having had things too easy in America for a long time. This may even be true in western Europe since the end of the Nazi era. During these years there have always been clergy who have preferred a simple life-style and have given of their own substance to help the less fortunate. But there have also been those who, in one way or another, took very good care of themselves. And there have been others still—a minority—who lived high on the ecclesiastical hog.

While there has been an admirable simplification of formal ecclesiastical appointments and other personal accessories (remember the big black cars parked by the rectory?), there is no doubt that the clergy, Catholic and non-Catholic, are quite comfortable. This is acceptable, but dangerous in times when the Church should be warning against materialism and consumerism. While the Catholic clergy earn very small salaries compared with their Orthodox, Protestant and Jewish colleagues, frequently they are materially very well off in the quarters provided for them. There are, however, cases of great inequality. I personally know young diocesan priests who do not have enough funds even to afford a well-merited vacation and must rely on family and friends to offer them hospitality. Others in the same diocese may be very well off. While no one can honestly say that there is any widespread cause for scandal regarding the life-style of American clergy, there is room for improvement. Some antidotes should be found for the materialism that is so deeply rooted in our culture. Not only must we not be any more materialistic than the rest of our fellow citizens, but we ought to be leading the way and reminding them of the clear teachings of Christ against worldliness. Is there an answer?

The Road out of Materialism

The obvious way out of materialism is generosity—starting with almsgiving to the poor and going on to many other acts of kindness. The Gospels, the Epistles and the lives of the saints from the earliest times until now offer a continuous call to generous giving. Many object that they have been taken advantage of by panhandlers at the door. This kind of incident represents only a small part of a Christian's obligation to be generous. In almost every parish, and certainly in every diocese, there are poor but gifted youngsters who need a better education than they are getting. There are needy elderly people who are on fixed incomes and families devastated by illness and death. There are immigrants and refugees who need the first boost up the ladder. Some will be grateful, and some will not. It makes no difference to the person seeking to grow in a spirit of repentance. How powerful a witness is a generous priest or minister! The most important thing for a generous clergyman to have is the willingness to open his eyes to see the needs of others in front of him.

At the present time the powerful voice for religion among all the nations and people of the world, even in countries of different religions or no religion, is Mother Teresa of Calcutta. I have been privileged to know this remarkable woman for almost two decades. The secret of her dynamism is not difficult to discover. She has absolute faith and trust in God and unbounded generosity. This gives her eyes to see what the rest of us miss. The following account will perhaps shed some light on the power of generosity to open our eyes to what we ought to see.

The Invisible Man

On a hot July day I was sent by Cardinal Cooke to bring Mother Teresa to investigate an abandoned church in midtown Manhattan as a possible shelter for the homeless. Accompanied by two other Missionaries of Charity, we were walking next to the long wall by the Port Authority Bus Terminal. When I arrived at the corner with the two other sisters, we looked up from our conversation to discover that we had lost Mother Teresa. Off in the distance, more than half a block back, I could see her bending over a figure on the sidewalk. I raced back to look into the eyes of a very frightened homeless man who had been asleep on the sidewalk when we went by. I think the poor soul thought that he was dead and had been awakened by an angel in eternity. He was only sleeping off a couple of drinks. I had walked past this man but had never even seen him. Mother Teresa, unfamiliar with this all-too-common sight in New York City, had thought the man was ill. Finally the man recovered his composure and laughed, and we all laughed with him. He was glad to be alive and not on his way to eternity. However, when this incident was over, I thought for a long time about the fact that I had never seen him at all, and I had passed within two feet of him.

As a nation becomes more materialistic, it becomes more and more insensitive to the plight of the poor, even the involuntarily poor such as children, the mentally ill and the aged. If the clergy do not give a powerful example of generosity, they will cease to be a prophetic voice and will be swallowed up in a worldliness that will numb their hearts and leave them spiritually dead.

The Teacher of Justice

The clergy of all spiritually oriented religions in East and West are expected not only to lead exemplary lives but also to live as witnesses to justice. In recent years, as part of the renewal, clergy have been in the forefront of prophetic movements for change. Since the early days of the civil rights movement, clergy and religious have become familiar figures in powerful causes such as racial justice, world peace and respect for the unborn. Perhaps this has been the most effective part of the whole movement for renewal springing from the Second Vatican Council.

But there are causes needing more of the clergy's attention that are minimally supported or all but ignored. The preservation and restoration of public morality is one of the clearest historical responsibilities of the clergy, going back to the time of the prophets of Israel. On almost every side one hears a consistent revulsion at the abuse of mass media as a force against sexual morality and human decency. One would have to be entirely insensitive to human decency and have a debased sense of values not to be offended by what pours out of the television sets of America. A whole generation of children and adolescents are growing up in an anticulture filled with sexual stimulation, hedonism (sex for fun), gender confusion and violence. The heaviest responsibility for raising an outcry against this falls on the clergy. Yet one hardly hears a voice.

More appalling is the utter lack of respect for human life. In fact, lives are constantly destroyed wholesale. Biological experiments that tamper with or destroy life go on with little or no moral evaluation. As we have mentioned already, the tragic failure of the scientific and medical professions to monitor their own experiments and activities in the mid-twentieth century has been examined by Robert J. Lifton.[7] In his book *Hitler's Doctors* Lifton recalls

---

[7] See Robert J. Lifton, *The Nazi Doctors* (New York: Basic Books, 1986).

that the prophetic voices raised against these abuses usually came from clergy and especially from the great Cardinal Von Galen, who was imprisoned at Dachau for his efforts.

The voices of the clergy in America against abortion, euthanasia and immoral biological experiments and procedures are weak and uncertain. Recently I gave a day of retreat to a very gentle and prayerful group of clergy from a large Protestant denomination. When I raised the question of abortion, all thirty ministers— without one single voice of dissent—agreed that it was a wretched and deplorable practice. One minister said, "It stinks." I asked what they were doing about it, and they answered that their church had officially taken a prochoice position. I was left wondering what the Catholic clergy would be doing if it were not for the Church's central authority, which fortunately is not dependent on the approval of those who support it. Several prolife speakers have observed that many Catholic high school and college students do not support the Church's teaching on abortion. They reflect the power of the media and public opinion to corrupt values. After all, abortion is consistent with our overall hedonistic amorality.

The clergy in the immediate future will need to be more and more prophetic and confrontational. They will be able to be so only if they lead lives of prayer and personal reform.

There are a number of other serious moral questions facing the Western nations. Such questions as our treatment of the poor nations, our concern for the homeless and growing underclass and the reduction of nuclear armaments will all need honest and careful moral assessment and action. Even in such areas of great controversy as the equal and just treatment of women, the rights and pastoral care of those who suffer from sexual deviation and the policy toward undocumented aliens and refugees, the clergy have to be ready to take a stand. We will know what to do and say as Christians only if our stand grows out of a life of prayer and personal reform. Otherwise we may become sounding brass and tinkling cymbals. Even if we give all we have to the poor and hand over our bodies to be burned, if we have not a personal love of God and our neighbor, we shall be nothing (1 Cor 13:1–3).

Chapter Ten

REFORM IN THE CHURCH AND IN SOCIETY

The Church, made up as she is of people, is constantly in
need of renewal and reform. Any living thing—be it a
plant, a human body or a social organism—needs constantly
to be renewed, or it will become moribund. Spiritual renewal,
when it occurs in human life and is done under the impulse
of the Holy Spirit, often is also a reform, that is, a return to
basic principles, a refocusing on basic goals. This process of
renewal in the Church is more or less constant over the
centuries, although there are times when the need for reform
is more obvious and intense. At times the Church needs a
deep and comprehensive reform, when a soul-searching
process of examination and change must take place. Such a
process may require several decades and is often the occasion of great conflicts and even schisms. The process of
major reform is most frequently begun when things in the
Church are in a very bad decline. Usually such a time of
major reform is also a period of activity by outstanding
saints, and we are reminded of Saint Paul's observation
that where sin abounded, grace did more abound. The
most startling example of such a reform in the history
of the Catholic Church was the conflict at the beginning of
the sixteenth century that led to the Council of Trent and the
Catholic Reformation. This was also the occasion of the

Protestant Reformation and the end of the unity of Western Christianity.

A Time of Major Reform?

The times we live in do not yet appear to me to demand a major reform like that of Trent. The Church is not in such a bad state as she was then. The last several Popes have been, without exception, men of genuine spiritual qualities and of great ability and compassion. No scandals have rocked the whole Church as they did in the age of the Borgias. No great outcry demanding reform echoes through the Church today. Despite much theological and political confusion, the basic structures of the Church, though challenged, do not appear to be crumbling as they were in the sixteenth century, when whole nations could leave the Church in a decade, thus reversing the loyalty of a thousand years. We do not yet seem to need a reform in the sense that saints from Catherine of Siena to Ignatius Loyola had to call for.

What we have lived through, in Arbuckle's words, is a revolution of expressive disorder followed by a period of cultural chaos.[1] This cultural chaos did not originate in the Church but, as it were, hit every structure in the civilized world, setting off reactions as diverse as the Red Guards in China and the hippies in the United States. At this writing in 1990, it appears again to be influencing the Communist countries profoundly. We have also lived through a time when the Church was attempting to adjust to immense changes in social life, especially the end of the aristocracy

[1] Gerald Arbuckle, *Strategies for Growth in Religious Life* (New York: Alba House, 1986).

and generally of the peasantry and the emergence of a predominantly middle-class society. Changes in politics, economics, international relations, science, technology and human thought occurred in the last one hundred years with tidal-wave speed. Only eight pontificates ago most European countries were governed by royalty. There have been only nine pontificates since the French ambassador to Italy sent word back that the last of the Popes, Pius IX, had just died.

The Second Vatican Council was a momentous and historical event pushing the ship of the Church away from the dock of western European civilization and preparing it, like no other large civil government has been prepared, for the coming of the age of supertechnology and a single economic world community. As disturbed as the Church is, she is probably better prepared for the twenty-first century than is any other world organization. Neither the capitalist nations nor the socialist countries in their varying degrees of communal economy appear even to be thinking of what to do in the new single world economy that comes upon us all for good or ill.

This statement of the Church's readiness may sound contradictory to what we have said with respect to the need for reform. The fact is that the Church as a whole may still need to continue the process of renewal, but she does not yet need an overall reform like that of Trent. What is needed very badly is reform *in* the Church, not *of* the Church. I will explain what I mean by this distinction.

Reform in the Church

This phrase is meant to convey that those who live in the Church need to reform their own lives so as to preclude the necessity for a large-scale reform of the Church in the future. The structures of the Church are not in a state of decay as they were immediately before the Reformation. The appalling examples of religious ignorance and superstition, the moral scandal and conflict that characterized the last decades before the Reformation do not exist today.

It is a sobering thought, however, that powerful voices for reform in the Church had been raised in the late fourteenth and fifteenth centuries before things became so bad. There were Catherine of Siena, whom we have already mentioned, and her fellow citizen Saint Bernardine. The fiery Savanarola had tried to call the Church in Italy to reform. In England and Germany spiritual writers of great prowess and lasting value were the mystics of the time. The authors of the *Imitation of Christ* and *The Cloud of Unknowing,* writers such as Julian of Norwich, Walter Hilton, Blessed John Ruysbroeck, Blessed Henry Suso and many others formed what Evelyn Underhill refers to as a network of spiritual believers in unbelieving times.[2] But they were not able to call forth a reform *in* the Church, so the reform *of* the Church became imperative. Sadly and for many reasons that had little to do with the teachings of the Gospel, the reform came too late.

[2] Evelyn Underhill, *The Mystics of the Church* (New York: Schockren, 1964), 153.

How Long Do We Have?

We live at a moment when reform in the Church is still possible and what is needed. How much time do we have before reform of the Church will be the only answer? How long will it take before moral confusion rises to the level of worldwide scandal, and the only way out will be through a powerful reformist spirit that will be vulnerable to becoming severe and repressive—a neo-Jansenism, which like the original would be a reaction to a time of moral decadence? How long will it be before unbridled theological speculation combined with widespread religious ignorance will spark a counterreaction capable of suppressing not only the erroneous but also the legitimately creative? Unfortunately, the fact that in the past it took the Church a century or two to arrive at a degree of decline requiring a full-scale reform does not at all imply that it will take as long now. Communications have accelerated the changes of history to an inconceivable speed. The rise and fall of the Nazis, the spread of the totalitarian systems and the significant reverses of apparently ironclad policies in Russia almost overnight suggest that powerful changes in direction can also take place in the Church in very short periods of time. Therefore, we do not have decades to decide whether or not we should pursue reform.

For all Christians in the Western capitalist nations the need for reform of personal life is imperative. To ignore this call is dangerous and might leave one at the end of life to face a charge of negligence and omission before the Lord Himself. This negligence might lead to inestimable spiritual damage and immense suffering for the generation that is being born right now. The frightening fact that large numbers of young people find the Church irrelevant and totally unchallenging suggests that the last chance of reform in the Church rather than reform of the Church is passing before our eyes.

Personal Reform: The Place to Start

In his *History of the Popes,* Ludwig Pastor credits a Genovese laywoman, Catherine Adorno (Saint Catherine of Genoa), with beginning the effective reform of the Church on the eve of the Reformation.[3] She lived in the worst of spiritual times. The attempted reform of the Church at the Fourth Lateran Council failed because bishops did not take seriously the call for reform and were embroiled in their own corruption and confusion. Although there were good Christians everywhere in the hierarchy, clergy and laity, there were so much ignorance, scandal and materialism that few seriously heeded the call to reform.

Catherine began a movement of personal individual reform called the Oratory of Divine Love. It was basically no more than a series of prayer groups, in which individuals strove to lead a good Christian life guided by the Scriptures and the lives of the saints and motivated to do works of charity. Catherine herself was director of a huge hospital for the poor. She died in 1511. Martin Luther was actually one of the many people who felt her influence and was struggling to work for the reform of the Church at that time. Catherine's work was not in vain, even though the split in Christianity came, because she

[3] Ludwig Pastor, *The History of the Popes from the Close of the Middle Ages,* trans. F. I. Antrobus, R. F. Kerr et al., as quoted in John C. Olin, *The Catholic Reformation: From Savonarola to Ignatius Loyola* (New York: Harper & Row, 1969), 16.

began the Catholic Reformation and even influenced the piety of Protestantism.[4]

Catherine's deep conviction was that reform had to begin with the individual. She lived in a time when the reform of the Church itself was needed. Not only were her prayer groups, or oratories, as they were called, very popular, but also her movement affected in one way or another almost every major Catholic reformer after her death. The great reformers of the Catholic Church in the sixteenth century all assumed that her basic principle was correct, namely, that reform had to begin with the individual. They all agreed that reform must be founded on prayer and expressed by charity to one's neighbor, especially the poor, and by love of God. All the Catholic reformers insisted on a deep personal piety, which psychologically galvanized all the potentials of the individual into action: intelligence, memory, will, emotion and even the intuitive powers.

Where Does the Individual Begin?

Clare of Assisi and Catherine of Genoa scarcely ever left their hometowns, and when they did, they stayed in the immediate neighborhood. They began where they were. Clare was led by Christ through Francis, and Catherine claimed to be led only by the Holy Spirit. They began their reforms right where they were, and they began with repentance and continued on with constant self-examination and reliance on God. Like the modern members of Alcoholics Anonymous, they acknowledged their powerlessness to do anything without help from above. They confessed that they were poor sinners, worked for others and made amends

[4] See S. Hughes, and B. Groeschel, eds., *Catherine of Genoa* (New York: Paulist Press, 1979).

for what they believed were their faults. As we mentioned in Chapter Two, the twelve steps of Alcoholics Anonymous (see Appendix One) are classic descriptions of any truly Christian conversion, including the conversion of these two great women saints.

Clare's poverty and Catherine's total dedication to the divine will are both reflections of the absolutism of repentance. Each speaks of the total desire to do God's will as it is known and to accept the vicissitudes of life as His permissive will. Both of these attitudes are reflected in the famous Serenity Prayer of Alcoholics Anonymous:

Prayer for Serenity

God, grant me the serenity
to accept the things I cannot change,
courage to change the things I can,
and wisdom to know the difference.

The absolutism of conversion—something that in itself goes against the grain of contemporary selfism—is perhaps best expressed in the total acceptance of God's will, which is the very heart of the poverty of Francis and Clare and the motivating force of the divine love of Catherine of Genoa.

Along with seeking personal reform in the various departments of life that we have outlined in the previous chapters, the individual must be willing to work to accept the divine will in all its mysteries. This is the key to true reform.

There are several powerful and brief classics of the spiritual life that describe this total acceptance. The writings of Julian of Norwich[5] and Brother Lawrence[6]

[5] Edmund Colledge and James Walsh, eds., *Julian of Norwich* (New York: Paulist Press, 1978).

[6] Brother Lawrence, *The Practice of the Presence of God* (Old Tappan, N.J.: Spire Books, Fleming H. Revell, 1978).

are fine examples of what Father Larranaga describes as the high-speed method to personal spiritual growth.[7]

Perhaps the most moving and intellectually powerful statement of the principle of acceptance of the divine will is *Abandonment to Divine Providence,* by Jean-Pierre de Caussade. This entire book can be read with great personal profit. The following quotation from this major classic can give the reader some idea of the force of personal reform that is at hand and that can be found in anyone brave enough to wish to follow Christ's call to repentance and reform.

The huge, unyielding rock that shelters the soul from all storms is the divine will, which is always there, though hidden beneath the veil of trials and the most commonplace actions. Deep within those shadows is the hand of God to support and carry us to complete self-abandonment. And when a soul has arrived at this sublime state it need fear nothing which is said against it, for there is no longer anything for it to say or do in self-defense. Since it is the work of God, we must not try to justify it. Its effects and its consequences will vindicate it enough. There is nothing to be done but let them unfold. If we no longer rely on our own ideas, we must not try to defend ourselves with words, for words can only express our ideas. So, no ideas, no words. What use would they be? To give reasons for our behavior? But we do not know these reasons, for they are hidden in the source of our actions, and from that source we have received only influences we can neither describe nor understand. So we must let the consequences justify themselves. Every link in this divine chain is unbreakable, and the meaning of what has happened earlier is seen in the consequences which follow. The soul no longer lives in a

[7] Ignacio Larranaga, O.F.M.Cap., *Sensing Your Hidden Presence: Toward Intimacy with God* (New York: Doubleday, 1987), 87ff.

world of thoughts, of imagination, of endless words. Now these no longer occupy it; neither do they nourish or sustain it. It no longer sees where it is going or where it will go. It relies no longer on its own ideas to help it to bear the weariness and difficulties of the journey. It carries on with a profound conviction of its own weakness. But with each step the road widens, and, having started, the soul advances along it without hesitation. It is innocent, simple and faithful and follows the straight path of God's commandments, relying on him, whom it meets continually along this path.[8]

Is There Another Way?

The diseases of materialism, selfism, cynicism and religious skepticism are so widespread and acute in our society and so pervasive in our culture that I do not believe there is any way other than personal conversion to work toward the reform of renewal. The Vatican Council's renewal was, as we have said, a very productive blessing. But the spiritual sicknesses of our time are destroying its good effects and turning its fruits sour and even poisonous. Deep-seated illnesses need radical cures.

We have lived through years of external changes and so-called reforms that have produced few spiritual results at the present time. Every conceivable aspect of Christian life has been questioned, reappraised, moved around and restated. The distressing decline of active church participation, the disaffection of large numbers of young people and the general spiritual apathy continue to grow. The time has come to stop talking and start on the long, painful road of personal conversion and

[8] Jean-Pierre de Caussade, *Abandonment to Divine Providence,* trans. John Beevers (New York: Doubleday, 1966), 109, 110.

reform. Then and then only can true reform happen in the Church.

Reform in Society

It has been one of the most important contributions of Vatican II to emphasize that a privatized spirituality with only token contributions to human growth and well-being is inappropriate for Christians. This emphasis by the Council and postconciliar spiritual writers has corrected some imbalance in the popular piety that preceded the Council. Nowhere in the Church has this change in emphasis been more obvious than in Latin America. A Christian spirituality unrelated to human needs, both spiritual and physical, is a contradiction of the Gospel, and no matter how austere and prayerful it is in itself, it is in need of reform.

However, societal reform is not the same as revolution or even reorganization. Both revolution and its more gradual counterpart, reorganization (like the New Deal of the 1930s), can flow from spiritual reform, but they seldom do. There are exceptional cases in Church history, such as the civilizing effects of Benedictine monasticism in the Dark Ages or the more limited reform of medieval society effected by Saint Francis and the whole peace movement of the friars and tertiaries. In contrast, the political upheaval of the nineteenth and twentieth centuries was scarcely the work of deeply spiritual reformers. As a result, the humanitarian goals often proposed by the organizers of the various revolutions were usually overshadowed by cruelty and the merciless severity that accompanied these reforms. One must recall that Robespierre, Stalin and Hitler all saw themselves as reformers of society. None of them had any values that were in the remotest sense spiritual; their revolutions were drenched with blood, and their reforms were contradictions of their stated goals. None of them had the slightest interest in any personal spiritual reform as described by the Gospel.

Occasionally political revolutionaries and reformers give evidence of values related to spirituality or the Gospel. However, I know of no case where any of these have spoken seriously of their own need for repentance and reform. However sincere their efforts, the results are often short lived and usually accompanied by bloodshed and arbitrary uses of power. Even in the stabilized governments of what is presumptuously called the "Free World", one almost never hears any suggestion that a leader ought to examine his conscience or admit his powerlessness to do anything good without the help of God.

Personal Reform and Societal Change

Modern society tolerates immense discrepancies between rich and poor, an atrocious lack of mercy to the unborn, a disregard for the physically ill who are indigent, a callous lack of protection of its youth against drugs and violence. This society desperately needs reform. There is a widespread fear in the intellectual world that we are heading toward global disaster, if not extinction. The individual feels powerless to do anything in the face of such overwhelming pressure. However, if even a relatively small number of people were to try to influence their own environment by following a Christian life of personal reform, change might indeed occur. It has long been alleged that

Lenin complained on his deathbed that if he had had ten men like Francis of Assisi he could have changed the world. What would the modern world be like if Lenin himself had tried to be one of the ten and had approached his career with the values of Saint Francis?

If there had been someone in Lenin's youth who had seriously embodied Gospel values as Saint Francis did, the world might be incomparably better today.

This writer has been personally convinced by a lifetime of work with the poor in what is called the richest city in the world that Western capitalist society desperately needs reform. Nothing I have ever heard has suggested to me that the Eastern bloc, despite its expressed goals, has any effective means of producing a societal reform to make life more decent and human for all. Is it too utopian to think that people seeking personal reform according to the teachings of Jesus Christ in the Gospel can effect some reform of society? Several important changes for the better in global human relations have been accomplished in this century by people who claimed to be motivated by a spiritual personal reform. Names such as Dag Hammarskjöld, Pope John XXIII and Mother Teresa come to mind. In non-Christian societies persons of spiritual values who confronted their own shortcomings and sought personal reform have brought about a number of positive social changes. Gandhi and U Thant provide outstanding examples. It is not unrealistic at all to suggest that a person seeking to express his own conversion in acts of justice and peace toward others can effect real change. In contrast, those who undertake to reform the world without first reforming themselves are likely to be at best sounding brass and tinkling cymbals and at worst blood-drenched tyrants and despots.

Challenge to Everyone

When we consider the serious problems in the Church and the magnitude of the dangerous conflicts and injustices in society, we can be simply appalled and completely intimidated. It is so easy just to walk away or hide in prayer and religious devotions and let the world go on its way to the apocalypse. This is not a legitimate way to follow the humble Carpenter Who, from the shore of a little lake in Galilee, started out to change the world. You respond, of course, that He had God on His side. So do we. But He was the only begotten Son of God. But, I reply, we are God's adopted children, and He Himself has promised to be with us to the end of the ages. Any great journey begins with one step and continues on with a momentum gathered with each succeeding step.

Mother Teresa once confided to me that if she had not picked up the first homeless man in Calcutta four decades ago, she would never have been able to help hundreds of thousands who are dependent on her and her sisters and brothers today. We have to start and keep going. We cannot all be Mother Teresa, but we can be who we are supposed to be. What we lack is the willingness to try and the trust to go on. I will not change the world or the Church—at least I hope not, because if I were to change them I would probably change them for the worse. Only God changes things for the better. But He does this through us if we give Him the opportunity to use us. There is no limit to how much God gives us except the limits that we put on Him by our self-centeredness and lack of trust. We must constantly be aware of the limits we place and must relentlessly push these limits back.

I once sat in a totally unpredictable place talking to a

person who has accomplished completely unexpected things for the kingdom of God. Mother Angelica, a cloistered Poor Clare, has developed a satellite television network, EWTN, adjacent to her convent in Birmingham, Alabama. With no regular source of income she provides religious television every day to millions of homes. Mother Angelica frightened me out of my wits by confiding, "Often, in the gray light of dawn, a chill comes over me. I ask what more I could have done if I had really trusted God." At first I thought that this was a touching humility, but as I thought about it I realized that she was right. We can always do more if we try to push back the limitations set by our own fears and shame.

Clare of Assisi no doubt heard from the friars the account of the last words of Saint Francis, "Let us begin now, because so far we have done nothing." She did begin again. So can I. So can you.

EPILOGUE

Conservatives, Liberals and Reform

There are many Catholics passionately interested in the renewal and reform of the Church. As a result of universal education and the relative disappearance of both the peasantry and the aristocracy and with the ascendancy of the middle class in all industrial nations, a much larger percentage of Catholics have opinions and personal concerns about the Church. This was brought home to me very directly when I recently attended a religious education conference sponsored by three dioceses in Los Angeles, with twenty thousand participants. A group like that generates not only many opinions but also a great deal of energy. No doubt widespread opinions on matters religious are not new in the Church. At various times in Church history there have been large numbers of people involved in Church decisions and policies. One thinks, for example, of the Crusades and the great crowds that followed the call of preachers. Saint Francis influenced very large crowds for his time. Saint Thomas Aquinas provoked riots. The Reformation brought out great multitudes on both sides.

However, it must be admitted that in the latter part of the twentieth century we probably have the largest percentage of Catholics involved in decision making and position taking in Church history. The problem is that this permits us to hide behind our ideologies and not to focus on our own need for personal change and reform. A person can follow the most sublime spiritual doctrine and be very energetic in promoting it and yet be cheating all the time. Apart from Judas, who was a case all by himself, we find Ananias and Sapphira cheating in the very early Church (Acts 5:1–11). Everyone thought that they were disciples of Christ, but they were cheating. We know little about those who opposed Saint Paul, for instance, the Galatians, but we do know that although they were Christians, they do not appear to have been living according to the Gospel.

In my own life I have been at one time or another styled as a liberal or a conservative, a radical or a traditionalist — just to mention the respectable positions. I have also been, in some people's estimation, a rat fink, a yellow rat, a pink, a leftist, a rightist and an undercover agent for the Swiss Guard. I blissfully hid from myself behind these rather meaningless designations. All the time I was really just a poor sinner.

Practically any position in the Church can be described in very virtuous terms. There are probably things to recommend almost any position at the present time, with some qualifications. However, we all too easily take the most virtuous expression of our particular position and the most debased description of the other side and proceed to console ourselves with the thought that they need reform and we do not. Now, at the end of this volume, I am going to risk alienating absolutely everybody by attempting to point out a few places where those who follow the more prominent ideologies might examine their consciences in terms of reform.

The Conservative Catholic

Since reform topics, such as the ones I have presented, are more frequently seen as the province of the conservative, I will start with some areas where conservatives might examine their consciences. Since conservatives generally support traditional morality, they can be lulled into the illusion that they live up to the morality that they espouse. Any spiritual director or confessor can tell you that this is not always the case. When it comes to vices such as pride, sensuality, lust and envy, the conservatives are just as good at them as is anybody else. Conservatives are often deeply distressed by profound feelings of guilt because their own lives do not match up with their loyalty to traditional Catholic moral teaching. Most decent Christians would not like to be hypocrites, so they are left with the alternative of either soft-pedaling their views and not saying anything about teachings to which they do not live up or perhaps changing their views arbitrarily when it suits them. If you are a card-carrying conservative, you know very well what I mean. Because the saints are part of Church Tradition, conservatives can generally marshal 90 percent of the saints in their defense. But when they look at the saints and how they lived, honest conservatives are frequently appalled because they are not living in the same way.

Conservatives also have a very fast trigger finger when it comes to innovation in the Church. They often overlook the historical fact that some of the Church's greatest innovators who earned the wrath of their contemporary Catholics are the heroes of the conservative movement at the present time. One need only mention people such as Saint Thomas Aquinas and Saint Alphonsus Liguori, who had their works vigorously condemned or brought into question, to see that conservatives ought at times to be more circumspect and gentle in their condemnation of the new.

Religious conservatism, particularly, lends itself to demanding of others what it is unwilling to do itself. I have known some people who are very conservative in their application of moral problems to other people's lives but who easily absolve themselves because of psychological compulsions or personality defects. They do not have the wisdom to recognize that other people who espouse a change in Church teaching are often different from them primarily because they are willing publicly to suggest the change. I am not suggesting in any way that the conservatives relinquish the defense of traditional Church teaching but rather that they begin as the Gospel suggests, by casting out the beam from their own eye.

Arrogance and self-righteousness have always been problems for those who defend traditional values. This was true in Our Lord's time of the Pharisees, who were trying to uphold the Law of Moses in the face of the rationalism and skepticism of the Sadducees. Loyalty to Moses did not stop the Pharisees from being tragically wrong about the Messiah.

Reform is everybody's job. It has a place in everyone's life. If you are a conservative and find that there are serious lacunae between what you believe and profess on the one hand and what you do on the other, it might be time to reevaluate your own genuine attempts at personal conversion. Be careful of absolving yourself too easily because you are an intellectual defender of what you take to be the cause of God.

The Liberals

Conservatives have no corner on self-righteousness. Liberal causes are associated in the minds of their adherents with the mercy and kindness of God, with the generosity and compassion of the Messiah and with a basic commitment to the idea that the Church is there to save souls and not to make things difficult.

Liberals generally look upon themselves as benevolent, kind, understanding and democratic. Anyone familiar with their track record in the last twenty-five years knows that these qualities are not necessarily universally found in liberal administrations. Having been burned at the stake by both liberals and conservatives, I maintain that I would always rather be burned by conservatives; they admit that they are doing it out of hate. When you happened to be burned at the stake by the liberals, you have to accept the ignominy of being burned out of love.

None of us is truly liberal or truly conservative in all ways. Those who style themselves conservative are usually willing to give up some very traditional positions that do not fit their own pathology or limitations. The liberals are also very quick to strike the liberal banner when it comes to a showdown with conservative opponents. They are no more likely to play a clean game than is anyone else. In America, *liberal* used to mean a respect for the other person's point of view. It has really come to mean progressive, or in favor of change. A very famous liberal, Father George Barry Ford, former chaplain at Columbia University, once commented to me in the early 1970s that there were no more liberals; there were only conservatives and radicals left. An examination of conscience might lead some liberals to ask themselves if they adopt certain problematic, or even questionable, theological positions because these are convenient. These opinions might not necessarily fit in with their own pathologies and temptations, but these positions could take the liberals off the hook of being witnesses to the hard sayings of the Gospel. I have known many liberals who are genuinely compassionate to others in their weakness but failed them when they needed to be led. Like the conservatives, the liberals also have the problem of being very selective about what is right or wrong.

If you style yourself a moderate liberal, it might not be a bad idea to ask yourself quite honestly how much respect you have for the other person's point of view. Are you actually willing to listen to that point of view and give the other person an opportunity to have his say?

The Arches

There are in the Catholic Church at the present time fairly large numbers of people on the far right and on the far left. They live under the arches, the banners of archliberal and archconservative.

Often these people have a prophetic sense. They have been willing at times to pay the price for their ideology. They have been ostracized, misunderstood, put in the back row, condescended to and treated like visitors from outer space. But they have not struck their colors.

Whether the arches are on the far left or the far right, they often feel that they have proved themselves disciples of Christ. They have won their spurs as knights in the cause of God. This is a very dangerous position, because along with being slightly paranoid, it convinces people that they are above the law. How many times have we all seen people, in the name of the Gospel, break the divine law, the natural law, the ecclesiastical law, the civil law and even the traffic code because they considered they were doing the work of God.

Since psychological pathology is rather evenly spread throughout the various segments of religious opinion, those who always take the high ground often have trouble living up to their own high ideals. Whether it be for peace, for life, for reverence in Church services or for involvement of the congregation in saving the old or hatching the new, whether it be in the name of God the Father, the Son, the Holy Spirit, or the Blessed Virgin Mary, or peace, or feminism, or creation, those under the arches are likely to see their cause as something so holy that it gives them permission to violate other people's rights.

Hatred of the opposition is not confined to either side. It is interesting to note that in religion hatred often carries some divine sign gathered out of the New Testament. Statements can be taken out of the context of the Gospel and can be construed to send this or that faction plumb to hell.

If you find in yourself a tendency to run for some of the arches—that is, to take some rather extreme point of view—it might be well to spend an hour in self-examination. The perfect Scripture quotation for meditation is the one cited above about seeing the mote in your brother's eye and not seeing the beam in your own (see Mt 7:3–5). I find that it comes in handy for a day of recollection.

The Moderates

The most interesting, varied and complex crowd of people gathered on the banks of the rivers of public opinion are those who consider themselves moderates. This is probably the majority of people in the Church at the present time. Although the name *moderate* would lead you to believe that it is a rather homogeneous and gentle collection, the fact is that the moderates include people of a wide variety of points of view. The moderates include those who would not like to be wrong, those who have been wrong so frequently in the past that they have given up having any opinions of their own, those who have overbearing parents or spouses, those who are trying to get ahead and do not want to offend anybody, those who are really not informed enough to have an opinion and not humble enough to admit it, those who are afraid to be wrong and, finally, those who have made it through life by always agreeing with the majority. There can be a quiet arrogance to the moderate position. It is a sobering thought for all moderates to remember that the position taken by Our Lord Jesus Christ was not considered a moderate one. Moderate people stayed home, or if they did come, they departed after He made the remarks about eating His flesh and drinking His blood. On the back of every temple of Apollo it is said that there was a sign encouraging people to moderation, but the Son of God said that the kingdom of Heaven is taken by violent assault.

It is so unusual for anyone to suggest that the moderate position might be a dodge for those trying to avoid personal conversion that it may even scandalize the reader that I am suggesting this. However, thoughtful moderates are often aware in a general way that there are less noble motives for their moderation. I suspect that in the gray light of dawn at least 50 percent of the moderates stare out the bedroom window and wonder if they have taken that position for the best of motives.

Anyone suggesting the need for reform in the Church should not omit the moderates from their audience. It was the moderates who let the Church get into its present position. These are not moderate times. There are challenges in front of the Church that are without parallel in recent centuries. The changes that had to be made were not moderate changes, and the adjustments that may have to be made now are not moderate adjustments.

While the arches may be arrogant and the liberals and conservatives may be doctrinaire and self-righteous, the moderates can be very smug too. It is wise for the moderates to spend time looking at their own sins. If we take the saints seriously, our sins are enormous. The mercy of God is infinite. It is not that our sins are picayune or unimportant and the mercy of God is simply moderate. The mercy of God does not say, Oh, it was all in fun, just a game, and boys will be boys. The mercy of God was won by the immoderation of the Incarnation, crucifixion and death of Jesus Christ.

Cool Comfort

As I reread the above paragraphs I was tempted to tear up this chapter. Ordinarily we make enemies on only one side of the ideological gap. Why make enemies on both sides? It was said of a certain national political leader who was known to be a devout Christian that he had a unique capacity for making enemies on all sides. Does this chapter do the same? I hope not. But I cannot be deterred by the possibility, lest I violate my conscience again by notions of human respect.

The fact is that ideology, no matter how sincerely

embraced and existentially correct, is no substitute for real personal conversion. I am not suggesting that liberals, conservatives or moderates give up their points of view. What would life be without them? I am not even suggesting to archconservatives and radicals that they depart from their positions. Would there ever be any real change if it were not for someone's extreme positions? Least of all am I suggesting that moderates abandon the pleasant plains in the middle. What relief would we have?

I am suggesting that we all need reform. We cannot dare pretend that our intellectual ideas will save us. That is gnosticism, which was condemned in the very early Church. It is such a stupid position for a Christian to take that one wonders if it even needed to be condemned.

The first question in any examination of conscience by someone who has strong ideological positions is, Do I live up to my position? Am I a traditionalist who defends all Tradition, whether I like it or not? Am I a liberal who is genuinely liberal even to those with whom I disagree? If I am a radical, do I really follow the radical ways of the Gospel? And if I am a moderate, does virtue for me lie in the middle, or do I simply lie down in the middle aisle?

The other questions included in this book focus on how personal, constant daily conversion applies to each one of us. If we are strong in our ideologies, we might also ask ourselves if we practice the virtue of charity. Do we love those who disagree with us? Are we willing to pray for them? Are we willing to give them the benefit of the doubt that they are, at least subjectively, operating with good motives? Are we open even to the possibility that they might tell us something? And finally, is our intellectual position truly a form of discipleship as Father Schnackenburg described it in an earlier chapter? Do we passionately embrace

Our Lord Jesus Christ as Our Savior and Lord? Or do we lackadaisically say, Well, I was born into this religion, and it must be right. Do we mistake a lukewarm Christianity for moderation and the prudence of the flesh for wisdom of the spirit?

All of these are painful and disconcerting questions. I ask them of you, dear reader, only because I have asked them of myself, and the answer that I always receive is the need for constant, personal examination and daily conversion. If by the grace of God I learn a few more things as time goes on, I suspect I may change this statement from saying daily conversion to saying hourly conversion.

CONCLUSION

A SIMPLE GUIDE TO
PERSONAL CONVERSION BASED ON
THE TWELVE STEPS
OF ALCOHOLICS ANONYMOUS[1]

Personal conversion for the Christian must be motivated by gratitude and affection for the Person of Jesus Christ, Who is present within us and around us in so many ways. Because Christ in His physical body is obviously not present to us—we cannot see Him or touch Him—we must use the powers of intelligence, will, memory and imagination to recall that His invisible presence is more real than the presence of any of those around us. Presence is largely a psychological phenomenon of response. We must work to respond to Christ's presence.

Jesus Christ, Present

Christ is present to us as the Word of God by Whom all things are made. This presence, sometimes called the Cosmic Christ, can be powerful if we personalize it, that is, if

---

[1] For an excellent guide to the Alcoholics Anonymous Steps for Everyone, see Philip St. Romain, *Becoming a New Person: Twelve Steps to Christian Growth* (Liguori, MO.: Liguori Publications, 1984).

we speak to Christ as we would speak to another individual. The old Crusaders' hymn "Fairest Lord Jesus", which recalls the beauties of nature, fields and mountains, is a fine example of personalizing the presence of the Eternal Word.

But through the Church, Jesus Christ becomes present in so many other powerful ways. He speaks to the believer through the prayerful reading of Scripture. He comes through the sacraments to those who receive them devoutly and reverently. His presence is centered and focused in the Holy Eucharist. This devotion, popularized in the Church by Saint Francis, is summed up in the historically authentic form of his prayer: "We adore You, Most holy Lord Jesus Christ, and we praise you here and in all your tabernacles throughout the world, because by Your Holy Cross You have redeemed the world."

Christ also speaks to us through the poor, the sick, the distressed. And sometimes He comes to us in the person of a loving and supportive friend. When we suffer, His consoling presence is as close to us as the image of His crucifixion. At the death of a loved one, His Resurrection shines in our hearts by faith.

We must direct the prayer of our repentance to Jesus Christ as a living, listening, responding friend. Otherwise, we may experience a personal change, but it will not be a Christian conversion.

Dependence on Christ

This realization of Christ's personal presence (corresponding to step 2 of Alcoholics Anonymous [AA]) leads to the next step, which is the acknowledgment to Him that without His grace we are helpless and lost. The members of Alcoholics Anonymous make their first step the admission of helplessness without God. For the Christian the admission of utter and absolute spiritual dependency must be directed toward the Savior: "Lord save me; I am perishing."

One of the most powerful prayers is to remain in the presence of the Savior, leaning on Him and accepting His strength. While other kinds of dependency can be counter-productive, dependency on God and His Son will motivate us to greater acceptance of our own responsibility for our lives if we heed the Gospel commands and counsels. Dependency on Christ must be honest. It requires not only that we say that we depend on Him but that—to paraphrase the twelve steps of AA—we make a decision to turn our wills and our lives over to His care. Many great spiritual classics have been written about this essential step of conversion, often referred to as complete trust, abandonment to Divine Providence or even perfect love. No one should become distressed if this step needs to be constantly repeated.

Moral Inventory and Repentance

For thousands of years spiritual writers of every tradition have required a fearless and searching personal moral inventory. Four (4–7) of the twelve steps of AA describe this process of self-examination, confession to another and prayer to God to remove our defects and shortcomings. A later step (10) requires the continuation of this process for the rest of our lives. For those fortunate enough to have a spiritual director, these steps are best made with this guide. For Catholics, sacramental confession presents a wonderful opportunity to receive the grace of forgiveness from Christ in a very explicit way. However, no one should think that a single and brief celebration of the sacrament of reconciliation provides all the psychological dynamism of a thorough confession. When the opportunity for a detailed and full discussion of our character defects is not available in the sacramental situation, one would be wise first to make the full account to a director and guide and then repeat it in a more succinct form in the sacrament.

Real Penance

Penance really means to make amends, to repair the damage we have done to God, to others and to ourselves. Penance means clearing up the debris left by our sins. The thought of all the evil that we can cause by our un-Christian behavior is so staggering that most people, even those who consider themselves followers of Christ, simply deny this responsibility. We all constantly visit evil on others and fail to do the good we could easily do. A persistent and contrite awareness of this need to repair and repay is part of any real discipleship and is summed up in a practical way in the eighth and ninth steps of AA.

Prayer and Meditation Necessary to Follow Christ

For the Christian, the eleventh step of AA reads something like this: We sought through prayer and meditation to improve our conscious contact with Christ, praying only for knowledge of His will and for the grace to carry it out. If we could do this perfectly, we would be on a short road to holiness. We need prayer and meditation to realize that there are many things we desire that have little or nothing to do with God's will. However, frequently we pray for the "grace" to do what we darn well please.

By a true, personal, daily repentance, we gradually become aware of what it means to accept and do the will of God. The perfect example of this loving acceptance is the life and death of Christ Himself.

Inspiring models of others doing this are to be found in meditation on the lives of Our Lady and the saints. Without prayer and insightful meditation, this process of conversion simply does not occur. Saint Clare and the other holy women disciples to whom this book is dedicated are sterling examples of this kind of prayerful and penitent discipleship.

The Good News

Every disciple of Christ is obliged to confess Him before all men and to follow His example. This is the real meaning of bringing the Good News to the ends of the earth. The lethargy, depression, conflictful attitudes and lack of commitment and zeal that are evident in the Christian churches at this time strongly suggest that no real sense of repentance and conversion is deeply present. There is no question that Christianity is losing ground because the Good News is not being effectively communicated to the people of our time or to young people who belong to families of faith. All those who consider themselves disciples of Christ must pause at this time to see if conversion is ongoing in their hearts. Every Christian is called to a ministry of reconciliation between man and God through the teaching and grace of Jesus Christ. We can hardly be working on this ministry of reconciliation for others if we are not pursuing it in our own lives. The real answer to the problems of the individual, of society and of the churches is to be found in the simple and direct words of Our Lord Jesus Christ at the beginning of His Gospel: "The time is come and the kingdom of God is at hand. Repent and believe the Good News."

Appendix One

THE TWELVE STEPS
OF ALCOHOLICS ANONYMOUS

This well known program of reform is included here because of my conviction that it summarizes in a popular way the steps of personal conversion. Although not an AA member I have profited greatly from attending open AA meetings for the past thirty years and have referred many people to the various Twelve Step programs which have grown out of the AA experience. These steps are solidly rooted in the Tradition of Christian spirituality and the teachings of the Scriptures and the saints.

1. We admitted we were powerless over alcohol—that our lives had become unmanageable.
2. Came to believe that a Power greater than ourselves could restore us to sanity.
3. Made a decision to turn our will and our lives over to the care of God as we understood Him.
4. Made a searching and fearless moral inventory of ourselves.
5. Admitted to God, to ourselves, and to another human being the exact nature of our wrongs.
6. Were entirely ready to have God remove all these defects of character.

The Twelve Steps reprinted for adaptation with permission of of Alcoholics Anonymous World Services, Inc.

7. Humbly asked Him to remove our shortcomings.
8. Made a list of all persons we had harmed, and became willing to make amends to them all.
9. Made direct amends to such people wherever possible, except when to do so would injure them or others.
10. Continued to take personal inventory and when we were wrong promptly admitted it.
11. Sought through prayer and meditation to improve our conscious contact with God as we understood Him praying only for knowledge of His will for us and the power to carry that out.
12. Having had a spiritual awakening as a result of these steps, we tried to carry this message to alcoholics, and to practice these principles in all our affairs.

Appendix Two

A MIRACLE IN MODERN TIMES

Of particular interest to our readers is the case of Vittorio Micheli, who was cured of sarcoma of the pelvis in May 1963 on the occasion of a visit to Lourdes. The following quotation is by Professor Michel-Marie Salmon, M.D., Professor of Anatomy and of Orthopedic Surgery, National Correspondent Member of the Academy of Surgery and of the Academy of Medicine of France.

> *To sum up,* Micheli had a malignant sarcoma of pelvis, with invasion of the buttock, destruction of the greater part of the ilium and pathological substitution of the hip joint. He was cured suddenly, without any treatment, and has remained well for eight years. Micheli's replies, by their conciseness, brevity and accuracy, reflect his truthfulness, later confirmed by his psychological, moral and even physical attitudes, which were never contradictory, showed no evidence of trickery and no desire for publicity. His modest way of life gave even greater emphasis to these remarks of convincing and indisputable value.
>
> In June 1971, Professor Merle d'Aubigne held a conference at Marseilles, where French and foreign specialists discussed papers on bone sarcoma. Here the Micheli case was presented as a case of spontaneous cure of the pelvis, no mention being made of Lourdes. Professor Nezelof of Paris confirmed the diagnosis, the details were discussed, but no one could offer a valid medical explanation of the cure. After a résumé of the case appeared in the *Journal of Orthopaedic*

Surgery, (57, no. 4 [June 1971], 323), this comment was made: "This is a quite extraordinary case where extensive destruction of the iliac bone ended in its reconstruction without any therapeutic intervention, except a biopsy. The histological slides nevertheless prove the existence of a malignant lesion of sarcoma of the pelvis in a sick man who went on pilgrimage to Lourdes as a last resort."

The publication of this résumé of Micheli's illness in an orthopedic journal of national and international repute constitutes something quite new. A few years ago, it would have been unthinkable that Lourdes should be mentioned in a highly scientific medical journal. At this stage, the cure is classed inexplicable, nothing else.

It is interesting for us to add to our report this epilogue, which confirms the objectivity of our work, of our conclusions and, above all, of our colleagues, whose goodwill and understanding have been for us the most rewarding recompense of our efforts.

The complete report on Vittorio Micheli can be found in *Lourdes, A Modern Pilgrimage,* by Patrick Markham (New York: Coward, McCann, Geoghegan, 1982), 198–216.

INDEX

Aaron, 20
Abandonment to Divine Providence, 193–94
Abraham, 19–20, 69–70
Akiba, Rabbi, 133
Alcoholics Anonymous, 123; as individual reform, 191–92; personal conversion based on, 211–16; twelve steps, 44, 217
Alphonsus Liguori, Saint, 202–3
America, 150
Andrews, Joan, 86–87
Angelica, Mother, 199
Arbuckle, Gerald, on chaos, 138–39, 186; on conversion and reform, 150–52; on decline in religious communities, 143–44; on Vatican II, 30–32
Arius, 62
Armstrong, Regis, 16–17
Augustine, Saint, 163; on analogies and divine reality, 66–67; conversion

of, 51, 55; on eros and love, 128, 129; on renewal and reform, 47–48; on repentence and reform, 174

Balthasar, H. U. von, 67
Becoming a New Person: Twelve Steps to Christian Growth, 211
Behold the Pierced One, 81–82
Belief in the New Testament, 69
Bell, Chris, 121
Bellah, Robert, 126
Bellow, Robert, 9
Bernardine, Saint, 188
Brown, Raymond, 76–77
Bultmann, Rudolph, 22, 113–14

Calvin, John, 65–66, 67, 68
Campbell, Donald, 96, 163
Casey, Solanus, 71–72
Catherine of Genoa, 58, 190–91

221